ตำราอาหารไทยในต่างแดน
ของ มลุลี (กุญชรฯ)ปิ่นสุวรรณ

Cooking Thai Food in American Kitchens
By Malulee Pinsuvana

ฉบับแก้ไขเพิ่มเติมครั้งที่ 3
Third Edition

PRINTING HISTORY

First Edition	First Printing	October	1976
	Second Printing	December	1976
Second Edition	First Printing	November	1977
	Second Printing	November	1977
Third Edition	First Printing	July	1979
	Second Printing	October	1981

ประวัติการพิมพ์

ฉบับแรก	พิมพ์ครั้งที่ 1	ตุลาคม	2519
	พิมพ์ครั้งที่ 2	ธันวาคม	2519
ฉบับแก้ไขเพิ่มเติม	พิมพ์ครั้งที่ 1	พฤศจิกายน	2520
ครั้งที่ 1	พิมพ์ครั้งที่ 2	พฤศจิกายน	2520
ฉบับแก้ไขเพิ่มเติม	พิมพ์ครั้งที่ 1	กรกฎาคม	2522
ครั้งที่ 2	พิมพ์ครั้งที่ 2	ตุลาคม	2524

Printed in Thailand by Thai Watana Panich Press Co., Ltd.

คำนำ

ตำราอาหารไทยในต่างแดน ฉบับแก้ไขเพิ่มเติมครั้งที่ 1 นี้ มิได้เพิ่มราย
การอาหารขึ้นมา หากแต่ได้เพิ่มเติมคำบรรยายและปรับปรุงข้อบกพร่องต่าง ๆ ของ
การพิมพ์ครั้งแรก และที่สำคัญก็คือได้เปลี่ยนแบบปกมาใช้ลวดร้อยแทนแบบปก
เดิมซึ่งหลุดง่าย

ตั้งแต่ต้นปี 2520 ข้าพเจ้าและครอบครัวได้ย้ายมาอยู่กรุงจาการ์ตา ตาม
สามีซึ่งมารับหน้าที่ในสำนักงานเลขาธิการอาเซียน อินโดนีเซีย เป็นประเทศที่อุดม
สมบูรณ์ในพืชพันธุ์ธัญญาหาร และมีอาหารซึ่งมีรสแปลกหลายประการ ข้าพเจ้า
หวังว่า เมื่อครบกำหนดกลับเมืองไทยในต้นปี 2523 จะสามารถนำเอาวิธีประกอบ
อาหารอินโดนีเซียมาเขียนได้บ้าง

ตำราอาหารไทยในต่างแดนพิมพ์ครั้งแรก ได้รับการต้อนรับจากท่านผู้อ่าน
ดียิ่ง ข้าพเจ้าขอขอบคุณท่านทั้งหลายมาด้วย ณ ที่นี้

มลุลี ปิ่นสุวรรณ์

1 พฤศจิกายน 2520

ตำราอาหารไทยในต่างแดน ฉบับแก้ไขเพิ่มเติมครั้งที่ 2 นี้ เพิ่มรายการอาหาร
หวานขึ้นมาอีก 8 อย่าง ในอนาคตอันใกล้นี้ ข้าพเจ้าหวังว่าจะสามารถเขียนวิธีประกอบ
อาหารจากประเทศอาเซียน ซึ่งรวมของอินโดนีเซีย, มาเลเซีย, ฟิลิปปินส์, สิงคโปร์
กับไทย ได้อีกเล่มหนึ่ง หลังจากที่ได้ใช้เวลาอยู่ในกรุงจาการ์ตามา 3 ปี และหวังว่า
ท่านผู้อ่านจะให้ความอุปการะเช่นเคยด้วยดี และขอขอบคุณมา ณ ที่นี้ด้วย

มลุลี ปิ่นสุวรรณ

31 กรกฎาคม 2522

คำนำ

  ความมุ่งหมายในการเขียนหนังสือเล่มนี้ขึ้นก็เพราะว่าเห็นใจคนไทย และ
คนที่ชอบอาหารไทยเวลาอยู่ต่างประเทศรับประทานอาหารฝรั่งไม่กี่วันก็เบื่อ อยาก
รับประทานแต่อาหารไทย ในต่างประเทศความจริงที่ประเทศไหนๆก็มีผักและ
เครื่องครัวต่าง ๆ ที่จะประกอบอาหารไทยได้ ไม่ต้องใช้ส่วนประกอบเหมือนที่เรา
ทำในประเทศไทยนักก็ได้ ข้าพเจ้าได้สะสมวิธีประกอบอาหารต่าง ๆ จากเพื่อน
และญาติ หลาย ๆ บ้านด้วยกันและที่คิดขึ้นมาได้เองก็มี ทุกปีเวลาโรงเรียนปิด
เทอมระหว่างเดือนมิถุนายน ถึง เดือนสิงหาคม ข้าพเจ้าจะท่องเที่ยวไปพักอยู่ตาม
บ้านเพื่อนทั้งไทยและเทศเป็นแม่ครัวให้ แลกทออยู่บ้านละห้าวันเจ็ดวันบ้างแต่ละ
บ้านแต่ละเมืองก็ได้วิธีทำอาหารมาหลายอย่าง ประกอบกับเป็นคนชอบทำอาหาร
มาแต่เด็ก คุณพ่อและคุณอาว์ทำกับข้าวเก่งมาก เป็นลูกมือมาตั้งแต่เด็ก ๆ พอแต่ง
งาน สามีเป็นคนชอบรับประทานจึงชอบทำมากขึ้นอีกและได้เคยคิดทดลองวิธีการ
ประกอบอาหารขึ้นเอง เมื่อติดตามสามีไปสหรัฐอเมริกาครั้งแรกเมื่อปี พ.ศ.
2506 - 8 และเมื่อมาทำการสอนอยู่ที่โรงเรียนนานาชาติ กรุงเทพฯ ก็ใช้เวลาหยุด
ภาคเรียนเดินทางไปเยี่ยมเพื่อนทั้งไทยและอเมริกันในสหรัฐบ่อย ๆ ก็ได้แสดงการ
ทำอาหารไทยเสมอ และสะสมไว้ได้มากจนคิดจะเขียนตำราขึ้นมา

  วิธีทำอาหารจากเล่มนี้เป็นวิธีทำแบบง่ายๆ สำหรับแม่บ้านใหม่ หรือนัก
เรียนที่มีเวลาทำอาหารน้อย หรือคนที่ไม่ชอบทำกับข้าวเลย จะเห็นว่าการประ
กอบอาหารไม่ยากเลย และสำหรับชาวต่างชาติที่เคยมาอยู่เมืองไทย และอยาก
จะประกอบอาหารไทยในต่างประเทศ

  ในการทำหนังสือเล่มนี้สำเร็จมีผู้อุปการะช่วยเหลือหลายท่านด้วยกันคือคุณ
เนาวรัชต์ ธรรมสโรช, คุณอัญชุลี อนันตกุล, คุณขจีวรรณ จิยจันทน์ ให้ขอยืม
ภาชนะสำหรับถ่ายรูป คุณชู สาลแวน, คุณมารี เรนีส, คุณซินเธีย อัศชว-
เมธี และมาดาม ไอลาลี อีเร็ท ช่วยขัดเกลาสำนวณและภาษาอังกฤษ ข้าพเจ้าขอ
ขอบคุณอย่างสูง ณ ที่นี้ด้วย.

                           4 ตุลาคม 2519

FROM THE AUTHOR

After having spent some time in the United States, I understand the longing of so many Thais living there for their native food. It is not that American food is not good, or that other types of food, Mexican, French, Italian and Chinese to name a few are not delicious, but their taste is not quite satisfying enough. In other words, Thais must have Thai food. My husband and I also have a wide circle of American friends, some that we knew in Bankok and others that we met in Phoenix and Los Angeles, who also love Thai food. The problem was always how to get all the necessary ingredients to cook a reasonable Thai dish. I encountered the same problem in Phoenix and in Los Angeles, but found it possible, after considerable experimentation, to solve it quite satisfactorily. This books is a result of those experiments. It is written for the many Americans who have been to Thailand and still remember Thai food. It is written also for many Thais who are studying or living in the United States. I have tried to use ingredients that can be found readily in any supermarket, but some items can be purchased at a Thai or Chinese store only. Most of these dishes are quite well known to many foreigners. Some dishes are, however, Thai specialties learned from my aunt, my father and my great aunt of the House of Kunjara in Bangkok, well known in the Thai Rayal Court and to the public in general as a famous family in the art of cooking, Thai classical dancing, and flower arrangement. As a matter of fact, one of the dishes I described was produced for Her Majesty Queen Elizabeth of England and her consort, the Duke of Edinburgh, on their visit to Thailand a few years ago.

The methods of cooking in the book have been modified to be simple enough for any new housewife or students with little time to spend in the kitchen. Experienced chefs, however, will enjoy cooking these Thai recipe also.

This book is dedicated to all our American Friends that we know from the U.S. Air Force Advisory Group in Thailand from 1962-68, General Research Corporation of Santa Barbara, OSD—ARPA Field Office—Thailand International School of Bangkok from 1966 to present, and USIS and US Embassy, Bangkok during all these years. We also dedicate this book to many of our friends in Phoenix from 1963 to 1965 and Los Angeles in 1973. You may find some of their names in parts of this book.

It took me about one year to complete this book and many friends have helped out greatly. Acknowledgement and gratitude is here given to Mrs. Nawarachta Thamsaroj, Miss Anchulee Anantakul. Mrs. Kache-evan Chiyachantana, Mrs. Raymond (Sue) Sullivan. Mrs. James (Marie) Raynis. Mrs. Cynthia Archwamety and Mrs. Paul (Ila Lee) Ehret who all provided substantial help to make this book possible.

Of course, I must say a few words for my husband, Capt. Adul Pinsu-vana (RTAF, retired) who has always encouraged me in cooking since we married, three children (for me) and twenty kilos (for him) ago, He insisted on making comments among the pages, so I shall be res-ponsible only for the part about cooking. We hope you will enjoy our cook book.

Malulee (Kunjara Na Ayudhya) Pinsuvana

October 4, 1976

SECOND EDITION NOTE

This Edition of the Cookbook remains very much the same as the First Edition. We have added comments to each of the dishes and corrected errors in the original text. We have changed the bind-ing of the book to solve the problem of its breaking apart.

In the early part of 1977 we moved to Jakarta where my hus-band took up his new position in the ASEAN Secretariat. Indonesia is a country rich in terms of fruits and vagetable and has a great variaty in cooking. We hope that by the time we leave Indonesia in January 1980 I shall be able to write on some Indonesian dishes.

We wish to thank the many who bought the First Edition and made this Second Edition possible.

MALULEE
November 1, 1977

Third Edition Note

For the Third Edition, I have added more recipes on desserts. Otherwise, it is still the same as the second edition. We hope to present a completely new cook book of Thai food with a special section on ASEAN dishes as a companion to this book sometime in the middle of the year 1980.

Malulee

June 30,   1979

สารบัญ

อาหารเช้า

กับแกล้ม

ก๋วยเตี๋ยว

อาหารหลัก

ของหวาน

CONTENTS

HORS D' OEUVRE

NOODLES

MAIN DISHES

DESSERT

ผัก

ผักต่างๆจะหาซื้อได้ตามตลาดไทย ตลาดเกาหลี ตลาดญี่ปุ่น และตลาดจีน ทั่วไป สำหรับหอมหัวแดงไม่จำเป็นต้อง ใช้หอมเล็ก หอมแดงหัวใหญ่ก็มีรสจัด และฉุน ถ้าจะใช้ทำน้ำพริกแกง ควร ลอกใช้แต่ชั้นนอก 3 ชั้นเท่านั้น เพราะ ชั้นในมีน้ำมาก และจะทำให้ตำเครื่อง แกงลำบากมักจะกระเด็น และควรจะหั่น ให้เป็นชิ้นเล็กเสียก่อน

ผักชี ล้างให้สะอาดเก็บไว้ในตู้เย็น โดย สะบัดให้สะเด็ดน้ำใส่ขวดปิดฝา จะเก็บ ได้เป็นอาทิตย์

ถั่วงอก แช่น้ำเก็บไว้ในตู้เย็นจะสดอยู่ ได้ถึง 3-4 วัน

พริกสดแม็กซิกัน ถ้าผ่าสีหั่นเป็นชิ้น เล็กๆ ร่อนเม็ดออกดองน้ำปลาแทนน้ำ ปลาพริกขี้หนูดอง

ใบแครอท เด็ดออกเฉพาะใบ ผสมกับ ใบผักชีตีกับไข่ใส่นมนิดหน่อยทอดแทน ชะอมชุบไข่ทอดรับประทานกับน้ำพริก

ผิวมะนาว ใช้แทนตะไคร้เวลาผสม เครื่องแกงได้

ใบสะระแหน่ ใช้แทนใบโหระพาและ กะเพรา และใบแมงลักเวลารับประทาน กับน้ำยา

VEGETABLES

Many of the vegetables used in Thailand cannot be found in the United States, I have tried to use substitutions and found that they worked very well

All vegetables in this cook book are available in the Thai Market, Oriental food stores, Spanish market, Japanese market or Chinese market nearest to you — — if you cannot find them in regular super markets.

ARTICHOKES May be used for ''Kratong'' (banana leafe cup) when you make Ho mok.

ASPARAGUS Boil and serve with ''namprik''. Also good when fried with shrimp and pork.

BEAN SPROUTS Soak in water. Will keep in refrigerator for 2-3days.

BROCCOLI Stalk—slice thin. Soak in water for 15 minutes, then fry in hot oil. Tastes as good as Chinese broccoli (Gailan choyor kana) or even better.

BRUSSEL SPROUTS Boil and top with coconut milk. Serve with namprik. Used in kang som (hot sour soup) they are delicious.

BUTTON MUSHROOMS Very good in curry.

CARROTS Grated carrots mixed with chopped cabbage make good ''som tum'' (papaya salad).

CARROT LEAVES Pick just the side leaves off the stem and mix with coriander leaves. Beat into egg with a few drops of milk. Pan fry like omelet. Cut and serve. (Good subsitute for cha—om tod.)

1

Vegetables

ก้านบร๊อคกอลี่ ปอกแช่น้ำทิ้งไว้ 15 นาที
ผัดไฟแรงรสอร่อยดีกว่าก้านคะน้า
ลูกสกว็อช แกงเลียงแทนบวบได้
หัวรัสเซิลสเปรา ต้มราดหัวกะทิจิ้มน้ำ
พริกอร่อยมากหรือจะใช้แกงส้มก็อร่อยดี
ก้านรูบาป หั่นเป็นแว่นผสมในแกงส้ม
จะช่วยปรุงรสเปรี้ยวและรสมะนาว คือ
ใช้แทนน้ำส้มมะขาม
แอปเปิ้ลเขียว ทานกับน้ำปลาหวานแทน
มะม่วงได้ หรือจะใส่ในแกงมัสมั่น
แทนน้ำส้มมะขาม

CAULIFLOWER Separate into flowe-rettes. Use in chicken curry. Cur-ry will remain thick and taste very good.

CORIANDER Wash thoroughly, re-move sand, drain well. Put in a covered jar. Will keep in refriger-ator for a week.

FRIED GARLIC Best to fry a lot of at a time and keep in a tightly closed jar. Used in many ways in Thai cooking.

GREEN APPLE Tastes much like the green mango.

ITALIAN SQUASH Very good for kang lieng. (Soup)

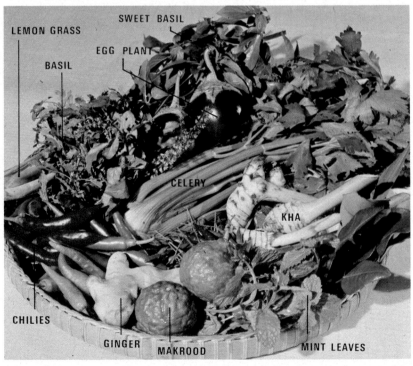

LEMON GRASS
SWEET BASIL
EGG PLANT
BASIL
CELERY
KHA
CHILIES
GINGER
MAKROOD
MINT LEAVES

2

วอเต้อเครส แกงบะช่อแทนใบตำลึง
ใบขี้นาจ ลวกแทนผักบุ้ง ทำเย็นโต
โฟ หรือพระรามลงสรง
ใบอ่อนของเชลเลอรี่ ผัดกับเนื้อปูหรือ
เนื้อปลาแทนขึ้นฉ่าย
เมล็ดถั่วลันเตา ใช้ใส่แกงแทนมะเขือ
พวง
ดอกกะหล่ำ หั่นใส่แกงเผ็ดจะไม่ทำให้
น้ำแกงใส ใช้ได้ดีกว่ามะเขือ
เห็ดกระดุมสด ใส่แกงเผ็ดแทนมะเขือ
แครอท ฝนด้วยที่ฝนเนยเป็นเส้นๆ ผสม
กับกะหล่ำปลีหั่นใช้แทนมะละกอ เวลา
ทำส้มตำ
หัวอาทิโช๊ก ใช้เป็นกะทงทำห่อหมกได้
กระเจี๊ยบ ลวกหรือเผา จิ้มน้ำพริกหรือ
แกงส้มได้
แอสปารากัส ต้มจิ้มน้ำพริกปลาร้าอร่อย
มาก หรือผัดกับกุ้งหมูก็ได้
กะชายแห้ง ข่าแห้ง ตะไคร้แห้งแช่น้ำ
อุ่นทิ้งไว้ 30 นาที ก่อนใช้
พริกดอง หั่นพริก ร่อนเม็ดออกเทหัว
น้ำส้มลงไปก่อนทิ้งไว้สัก 15 นาทีจึงเติม
น้ำจะทำให้พริกดองกรอบน่ารับประทาน

กระเทียมเจียว ควรเจียวใส่ขวดไว้ทีละ
มากๆ พอเวลาจะใช้ผัดหรือใส่ก๋วยเตี๋ยว
จะใช้ได้ทันที ไม่ต้องเจียวทุกครั้ง

KRACHAI, LEMON GRASS, and **KHA** (Dried) Soak in warm water for 30 minutes before use.

LEMON–PEEL May be used instead of lemon grass when you make curry paste.

MEXICAN CHILI Cut lengthwise in fourths and chop into small segments. Strain out seeds. Put chili segments in nampla (fish sauce). Tastes as good as nampla–prik keeno in Thailand.

MINT LEAVES Put into curry instead of sweet basil or basil and serve with "namya" in place of bai mang luck.

OKRA Boil or roast. Serve with "namprik" or use in kang som (hot & sour soup).

PICKLED CHILI Cut chilies and remove seeds. Add vinegar and let stand for 15 minutes. Add water and let stand for one hour. Serve with all kinds of noodles. Will keep for months in a covered jar.

RED ONION Substition for shallots. Use only the first three layers of the red onion, They are stronger and drier. But before use, chop up very fine.

RHUBARB Cut into small pieces. Mix with other vegetables in kang som (hot–sour soup).

SPINACH Use in place of "puk boong" (morning glory).

SWEET PEAS Put in all kinds of curry in place of "ma kua pong" (small egg plant).

WATER CRESS Put in ground pork soup instead of "Bai Tumlung".

YOUNG CELERY LEAVES Fry with crabmeat or sliced fish. Tastes just like Chinese celery.(bai kuan chai).

3

Glossary

เครื่องครัว

ผงชูรส อายิโนะโมะโต๊ะและ อีกชื่อ
หนึ่งว่า แอคเซ่น หาซื้อได้ในตลาด
ทั่วไป

เต้าหู้ หาได้ง่ายในตลาดจีนทั่ว ๆ ไป
เรียกว่า บีนเค็ก ใส่กล่องแช่น้ำไว้อัน
ใหญ่ขนาด 3″×3″ ฟองเต้าหู้เป็นแผ่น
ใหญ่ๆ คล้ายข้าวเกรียบว่าว

GLOSSARY

Ac'cent, Ajinomoto — Monosodium glutamate (MSG.)

BEAN CURD (Taw Hou) A soft white cake made from Soybeans that is similar in texture to cheese. Dried bean curd usually comes in twists or flat sheets. Fresh, dried and canned varieties can be purchased in all Oriental food shops. Bean curd squares are usually 3″ square.

BEAN CURD (Taw hu)
HOI SIN SAUCE
TARO
BROWN BEAN SAUCE
PICKLED LETTUCE
BAMBOO SHOOTS
BEAN CAKE
DRIED FISH (Pla-grob)

เต้าเจี้ยว เรียกว่า "บราวน์ บีนซ๊อส"
มีทั้งใส่ขวดและขนาดกระป๋อง ๆ ละ 8
ออนซ์ มีขายตามตลาดจีน

เห็ดหอม เรียกว่า "ดราย แบล็คมัช
รูม" มีขายตามตลาดจีน, ตลาดญี่ปุ่น
ควรแช่น้ำอุ่นก่อนปรุงอาหาร

หน่อไม้ มีขายเป็นกระป๋องขนาด 17
ออนซ์ มีรสจืด เหมือนหน่อไม้ไผ่ตง

เส้นบะหมี่ บะหมี่สด มีขายตามร้าน
จีน และตลาดญี่ปุ่น แต่เส้นใหญ่กว่า
ของบ้านเรามาก

ช๊อสหมูแดง มีทั้งกระป๋องและขวดชื่อ
"ฮอย ซิน ซ๊อส" มีขายตามร้านชำ
ของจีน

ก๋วยเตี๋ยว มีทั้งเส้นเล็กและเส้นใหญ่
และเป็นแผ่นใหญ่ๆด้วยแต่แผ่นหนากว่า
ของที่ขายในเมืองไทย มีขายตามร้าน
ขายของจีน

น้ำกะทิ มะพร้าวลูก ๆ มีขายทั่วไปใช้
บดในเครื่องบดอาหารเติมน้ำร้อน 2 ถ้วย
ต่อมะพร้าวขูด 1 ถ้วย ทิ้งไว้สักครึ่ง
ชั่วโมงแล้วจึงคั้น มีน้ำกะทิสำเร็จขาย
ขนาดกระป๋องละ 8 ออนซ์ หาได้ใน
แผนกของแช่เย็น สำหรับน้ำกะทิที่ใช้
ทำขนมควรใช้มะพร้าวกระป๋อง เรียกว่า

BROWN BEAN sauce A sauce with the consistency of ketchup, made of crushed soy beans, chilies, garlic and salt. It is available in bottles or 8 ounce cans; may be purchased in Oriental food stores.

BLACK MUSHROOM Dried whole mushrooms with very dark skin are stronger in flavor than the white mushrooms. It gives a distinctive taste to the dishes in which it is used. Before cooking they must be soaked in warm water until soft. Available in any Oriental store.

BAMBOO SHOOTS Bamboo sprouts packed in water. They are available in 17 ounce cans.

BA–MEE Egg noodles. Available in Chinese markets.

COCONUT MILK Scrape the meat from a fresh coconut. A blender is very useful for grating coconut. Add 2 cups hot water to each cup coconut meat. Let stand for half an hour, then squeeze through cheesecloth or strainer to extract the milk. Also 18 ounce packets of coconut frozen are available in the frozen food section in all supermarkets.

FOR MAKING Thai dessert, may use "Baker's Angel Flake" coconut available in all super markets. Add $\frac{1}{2}$ cup hot water to each can ($3\frac{1}{2}$ ounce) of coconut meat. Let stand for half an hour. Squeeze and strain.

CURRY PASTE Comes in envelopes available at Thai and some special Chinese markets.

Glossary

On this page you see the many different kinds of noodles used in the recipes in this book. In most cases they can be substituted one for another, except for wun sen and won ton.

The names can be spelled in so many ways that we have not tried to be consistent throughout the book.

We hope the picture will help you to identify whatever is available in your markets.

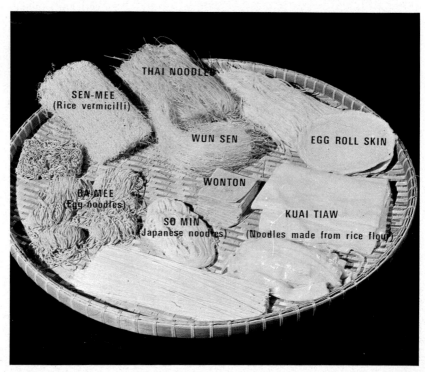

แองเจิลเฟลค ของเบเกอร์ คั้นด้วยน้ำ
ร้อนครึ่งถ้วย ต่อมะพร้าว 1 กระป๋อง
กะบิ ตามร้านจีนต่าง ๆ เรียกว่าซรัมเพส
กุ้งแห้ง มีขายทั่วไปแม้แต่ตามซูเปอร์-
มาเก็ต อยู่แถวเครื่องเทศมีทั้งบนและ
เบนตัวแต่แห้งมากควรจะแช่น้ำทิ้งไว้สัก
15 นาทีก่อนใช้

ผิวมะกรูดและใบมะกรูด ในตลาดไทย
หาซื้อได้เป็นห่อ ๆ ตากแห้งแล้ว ควร
แช่น้ำก่อนทำเครื่องแกง แต่ถ้าหาไม่ได้
ใช้ผิวมะนาวแทนก็ได้

ตะไคร้ มีขายทั้งสดและแห้ง ตามตลาด
จีนและ ตลาดไทย ถ้าหาไม่ได้ ใช้ผิวมะ
นาวขูดแทนได้ดี

น้ำปลา ทิพรสของไทยก็แพร่หลายมาก
ถ้าไม่มี ของจีน หรือ ของฟิลิปปินส์ก็ดี
เหมือนกัน เขาเรียกกันว่า พืชซ๊อส

ครก ครกแม็กซิกันมีขายอยู่บ้างตามร้าน
แม็กซิกันแต่ทำด้วยไม้ แต่ใช้เครื่อง
บดอาหารดีกว่าเติมน้ำนิดหน่อย เวลาบด
เครื่องแกง

น้ำมันหอย มีขายทั้งเป็นกระป๋องและ
ขวดเรียกว่า "ออยสเต้อซ๊อส" หาง่าย
ตามตลาดจีน

กระชาย–ข่า มีขายเป็นถุงตากแห้ง
ตามตลาดไทยควรแช่น้ำอุ่นก่อนใช้

DRIED SHRIMP Small sun dried
shrimp must soak in hot water for
15 minutes before using. Available
in Oriental food markets.

HOI SIN SAUCE Chinese Bar–B–Q
sauce, available in Chinese food
shops.

KAPI Available at the Chinese
markets in paste or powder from
Philippine markets, also in cans
called baggong. If not, it can be
substituted with anchovy paste, but
use only half the amount.

KHA Looks like ginger root. May
be purchased in a package, dried.
Available in Thai markets.

KRA–CHAI Similar to ginger root.
May be purchased in a package,
dried. Available in Thai markets.

KUAI TIAW Noodles made from
rice flour. Comes In small and big
strips. Available in special Chinese
food stores.

LEMON GRASS May be purchased
in powder form from any Oriental
specialty food shops. One teaspoon
equals one stalk of fresh lemon
grass. If neither fresh nor powder
is available, substitute a thin slice
of lemon peel, grated.

MAKRUT LEAVES Dried leaf of a
wild lime tree, used as seasoning.
Lime rind may be substituted.

MORTAR & PESTLE Use electric
blender — follow instructions on
grinding vegetable.

7

Glossary

In a Thai home, if you do not have one or two sets of mortar and pestle you do not have a proper kitchen. The best mortars are made from a solid piece of rock, the pestles from hard wood. With airtravel weight restrictions, few Thais can take this proper kitchen equipment abroad. But an electric blender can be used with very good results. Take care to clean it thoroughly, for Thai food is definitely not to be mixed with cocktails or milkshakes.

MORTAR & PESTLE

TAMARIND

PALM SUGAR

K'AMIN

COCONUT

KRACHAI

GARLIC

RED ONION OR SHALLOTS

DRIED CHILI

น้ำตาลบึก บางทีหาได้ตามตลาดแม็ก
ซิกันเรียกว่า "ปาล์มซูการ์" แต่ใช้น้ำ
ตาลสีรำแทนก็ได้

พริก พริกของแม็กซิกันชื่อ "จาลาพีโน"
เผ็ดดีจริง ๆ มีขายตามตลาดจีนและตลาด
แม็กซิกันทั่วไป

สาคู ควรซื้อที่ตลาดจีน เพราะของฝรั่ง
ไม่ค่อยเหนียว ทำสาคูไส้หมูไม่ได้ เรียก
ว่า "แท็ปปีโอก้า"

ข้าวเหนียว เรียกกันว่า "สวีทไร้" ของ
ญี่ปุ่นเม็ดอ้วน ๆ สั้น ๆ มีขายตามร้าน
ญี่ปุ่นและตลาดจีน

ซีอิ๊ว ซีอิ๊วญี่ปุ่นมีขายทั่วไปแต่เป็นซีอิ๊ว
ใสถ้าต้องการซีอิ๊วข้นต้องซื้อที่ตลาดจีนมี
ทั้งขวด และเป็นกระป๋อง

เส้นหมี่ มีขายตามร้านจีนเรียกว่า "ไหม
ฝืน"

ส้มมะขาม นอกจากตลาดไทยบางทีหา
ได้ตามตลาดแม็กซิกันเรียกว่า "แทมมา
เรนพอด"

กะทะก้นลึก มีขายตามตลาดจีนเรียกว่า
"ว๊อค"

วุ้นเส้น มีขายตามร้านจีนและญี่ปุ่นเส้น
ใหญ่กว่าของบ้านเรา

เครื่องแกง มีขายที่ตลาดไทย และตลาด
จีนบางแห่ง เป็นซอง ๆ

NAMPLA A fish sauce. Available as fish sauce in Chinese and specialty food shop.

OYSTER SAUCE Extract from oyster, soy sauce and cornstarch. Available in Chinese and specialty food shops.

PALM SUGAR Available at the Spanish markets or may use light brown sugar.

PRIK Hot chilies and pepper or use Jalapeno peppers.

SWEET BASIL May be substituted by using mint leaves.

STICKY RICE Glutinous—sweet rice. May be obtained in Chinese markets.

SEN—MEE Rice vermicelli. Under the name of Mai—Fun, available in Chinese markets.

SAKU Tapioca.

SOY—SAUCE Japanese soy sauce is always dark in color. Chinese soy sauce comes in light and dark varieties and the type used depends upon the other ingredients in the recipe. The dark is more bitter.

TAMARIND PODS Available in Spanish markets.

WOK A bowl—shaped metal pan for stir—frying foods. May be purchased at American and Chinese stores.

WUN SEN It is a transparent vermicelli, made from mung beans.

Curry pastes

The heart of Thai cooking is the curry paste. It is a family tradition to pass on the skill of blending various types of curry pastes from mother to daughter. For those modern young ladies who no longer consider cooking an integral part of proper upbringing, different kinds of curry pastes are available, precooked, as shown in this picture.

However, curry pastes are not hard to mix by yourself if you try. The fresh taste and smell much better than those from a package. I hope you will not be too modern and will try to prepare your own paste.

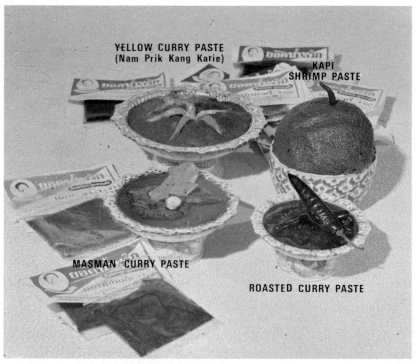

YELLOW CURRY PASTE
(Nam Prik Kang Karie)

KAPI
SHRIMP PASTE

MASMAN CURRY PASTE

ROASTED CURRY PASTE

๑. น้ำพริกแกงส้ม

ส่วน

พริกแห้งหรือพริกสด	10	เม็ด
หัวหอมแดงหั่น	1 ½	ช้อนโต๊ะ
กะปิ	1	ช้อนโต๊ะ
เกลือ	1	ช้อนโต๊ะ

วิธีทำ

ผ่าพริกแกะเม็ดออก ถ้าใช้พริกแห้งแช่น้ำทิ้งไว้สัก 10 นาที บีบให้สะเด็ดน้ำ แล้วตำกับหัวหอม และเกลือใส่กะปิเป็นอย่างสุดท้าย

๒. น้ำพริกเผา

ส่วน

พริกแห้งแกะเม็ดออก	10	เม็ด
หอมแดงหั่นเป็นชิ้นเล็ก ๆ	2	ช้อนโต๊ะ
กระเทียมหั่น	1	ช้อนโต๊ะ
กุ้งแห้งบ่น	2	ช้อนโต๊ะ
น้ำปลา	1	ช้อนโต๊ะ
น้ำตาล	1	ช้อนโต๊ะ
น้ำมัน	2	ช้อนโต๊ะ

วิธีทำ

เผาพริกแห้ง หอม กระเทียมให้สุก (ห่อกระดาษตะกั่วย่างบนเตาแก๊สหรือเตาไฟฟ้า) แล้วตำให้ละเอียดใส่กุ้งแห้งบ่นตำต่อไปจนเข้าเนื้อกันดี ตั้งกะทะใช้ไฟอ่อน ๆ ใส่น้ำมันพอร้อนผัดพริกจนหอม ปรุงด้วยน้ำปลาน้ำตาล

ORANGE CURRY PASTE
(Som)

INGREDIENTS:

10 dried or fresh chilies
1½ tablespoons chopped red onion
1 tablespoon kapi (shrimp paste)
1 teaspoon salt

METHOD:

Remove seeds from chilies. Soak the pods in cold water, then pound fine with salt, add red onion and kapi last of all.

ROASTED CURRY PASTE
(Pow)

INGREDIENTS:

10 dried chilies
2 tablespoons chopped red onion
1 tablespoon chopped garlic
2 tablespoons pounded dried shrimp
1 tablespoon sugar
1 tablespoon nampla (fish sauce)
2 tablespoons vegetable oil

METHOD:

Use aluminium foil and wrap dried chilies, red onion, and garlic in package place directly on the stove burner, until cooked about 2 mins. on each side pound, then add dried shrimp. In a frying pan heat the oil ; fry the paste until brown. Season with sugar and nampla.

Curry pastes

๓. น้ำพริกแดง

ส่วน

พริกแห้ง	7-10	เม็ด
ยี่หร่า	2	ช้อนชา
ลูกผักชี	1	ช้อนชา
ผิวมะกรูดหั่นละเอียด	$\frac{1}{2}$	ช้อนชา
เกลือ	1	ช้อนชา
ตะไคร้หั่นฝอย	2	ช้อนโต๊ะ
หอมแดงหั่น	$1\frac{1}{2}$	ช้อนโต๊ะ
กระเทียมหั่น	1	ช้อนโต๊ะ
ข่าหั่นฝอย	1	ช้อนโต๊ะ
กะปิ	1	ช้อนโต๊ะ

วิธีทำ

คั่วลูกผักชียี่หร่าในกะทะจนเหลือง เท
ใส่ครกตำให้ละเอียดพักไว้ ผ่าพริกแห้ง
แกะเม็ดแช่น้ำทิ้งไว้ 2-3 นาที บีบน้ำ
ออกตำกับเกลือให้ละเอียด เติมตะไคร้
ข่า ผิวมะกรูด ตำต่อไปอีก เติมหัวกระ
เทียม หัวหอมเมื่อแหลกดีแล้วใส่กะปิ
แล้วผสมด้วยลูกผักชียี่หร่าบ่น

RED CURRY PASTE
Kang Pet (Dang)

GREEN CURRY PASTE
(Kang Kiew Warn)

ORANGE CURRY PASTE
(Som)

4. น้ำพริกแกงเขียวหวาน

ส่วน

พริกเขียวสด	10	เม็ด
ตะไคร้หั่น	2	ช้อนโต๊ะ
รากผักชีหั่น	1	ช้อนชา
หัวหอมแดงหั่น	1	ช้อนโต๊ะ
กระเทียมหั่น	1	ช้อนโต๊ะ
ข่าหั่น	1	ช้อนชา
ลูกผักชี	1	ช้อนชา
ยี่หร่า	1	ช้อนชา
พริกไทย	7	เม็ด
เกลือ	1	ช้อนชา
กะปิ	1	ช้อนชา

วิธีทำ

คั่วลูกผักชียี่หร่าพอเหลือง เทใส่ครกตำ
ให้ละเอียดพักไว้ เครื่องปรุงทุกอย่าง
ยกเว้นกะปิเทใส่กะทะคั่วพอสุกใส่ครก
ตำให้ละเอียดดีแล้วเติมกะปิ แล้วผสม
ด้วยลูกผักชียี่หร่าป่น

5. น้ำพริกแกงกะหรี่

ส่วน

พริกแห้ง	7	เม็ด
ลูกผักชี	1	ช้อนชา
ยี่หร่า	1	ช้อนชา
อบเชยบ่น	$\frac{1}{2}$	ช้อนชา
ก้านพลูบ่น	$\frac{1}{2}$	ช้อนชา

RED CURRY PASTE
Kang Pet (Dang)

INGREDIENTS :
7—10 dried big chilies
2 teaspoons caraway seeds (yirah)
1 teaspoon coriander seeds (look phuk she)
$\frac{1}{2}$ teaspoon makrud rind (optional— see glossary) 1 teaspoon salt
2 tablespoons chopped lemon grass or lemon peel
1 tablespoon chopped kha (optional)
$1\frac{1}{2}$ tablespoons chopped red onion (shallot)
1 tablespoon chopped garlic
1 tablespoon kapi (shrimp paste)

METHOD :
Brown caraway and coriander seeds over low heat (without oil) ; cool then pound and set aside.

Remove seeds from the chilies. Soak the pods in cold water, then pound fine with salt. Add other ingredients in order. Pound very fine, then mix with caraway and coriander powder.

GREEN CURRY PASTE
(Kang Kiew Warn)

INGREDIENTS :
10 fresh green chilies
2 tablespoons chopped lemon grass or lemon peel
1 teaspoon chopped coriander root
1 tablespoon chopped red onion (shallot)
1 tablespoon chopped garlic
1 teaspoon chopped kha (see glossary)
1 teaspoon pounded coriander seeds

หัวหอมหั่น	2	ช้อนโต๊ะ
กระเทียมหั่น	1	ช้อนโต๊ะ
ตะไคร้หั่น	1	ช้อนโต๊ะ
เกลือป่น	1	ช้อนชา
ผงกะหรี่	1	ช้อนโต๊ะ
ผงขมิ้น	1	ช้อนชา

วิธีทำ

คั่วลูกผักชี่หร่าพอเหลือง เทใส่ครกตำ
ให้ละเอียดพักไว้ แกะพริกแห้งแช่น้ำไว้
สัก 2-3 นาที บีบขั้นจากน้ำใส่ครกตำ
กับเกลือพอละเอียด ใส่เครื่องเทศทั้ง
หมดตำต่อไปจนละเอียด ผสมด้วยลูก
ผักชี่หร่าป่น

6. น้ำพริกแกงมัสมั่น

ส่วน

พริกแห้ง	7-10	เม็ด
ข่าหั่น	1	ช้อนโต๊ะ
ลูกผักชี่หร่า	2	ช้อนโต๊ะ
ตะไคร้หั่น	1	ช้อนชา
เกลือ	1	ช้อนชา
ก้านพลู	5	ก้าน (ป่น 1 ช้อนชา)
อบเชย	1	แท่ง
หอมแดงหั่น	2	ช้อนโต๊ะ
กระเทียม	5	กลีบ
ลูกกะวาน	5	ลูก
กะปิ	1	ช้อนชา

14

1 teaspoon pounded caraway
seeds
7 white pepper—corns
1 teaspoon salt
1 teaspoon kapi (shrimp paste)

METHOD :

Stir—fry all ingredients except
kapi in saucepan. Then put all ingredients into a mortar and pound
until a smooth paste.

NOTE : You may use a blender, adding a little water to ease
grinding.

YELLOW CURRY PASTE
(Nam Prik Kang Karie)

INGREDIENTS:

7 dried chilies
1 teaspoon coriander seeds
1 teaspoon caraway seeds
$\frac{1}{2}$ teaspoon cinnamon
$\frac{1}{2}$ teaspoon cloves
2 tablespoons chopped red onion
1 tablespoon chopped garlic
1 tablespoon chopped lemon
grass
1 teaspoon salt
1 tablespoon curry powder
1 teaspoon dry mustard.

METHOD:
Cook coriander seeds and caraway
seeds in a fry pan over a low heat
(without oil) until brown. Cool, then
pound and set aside.
Remove seeds from the chilies. Soak
the pods in cold water, drain then
pound, add all other ingredients
and pound until very fine.
Then mix with pounded coriander
and caraway.

MASMAN CURRY PASTE

INGREDIENTS:

7—10 dried chilies
1 tablespoon kha (see glossary)

ใบกะวาน　　　　5　ใบ
น้ำมันพืช　　　　2　ช้อนโต๊ะ

วิธีทำ

เผากระเทียมกับหัวหอมแบ่งไว้ต่างหาก
แกะพริกแห้งแช่น้ำและตัดเป็นชิ้นๆ นำ
เครื่องแกงทุกอย่าง (ยกเว้นลูกกระวาน
ใบกะวานและกะปิ) คั่วในกะทะพอสุก
นำมาโขลกพอละเอียดดี เติมหอมเผา กระ
เทียมเผาและกะปิ ตั้งกะทะใส่น้ำมันผัด
เครื่องแกงใช้ไฟอ่อนๆ จนหอม ใส่ลูก
กระวานใบกระวาน

7. น้ำจิ้มสะเต๊ะ

ส่วน

น้ำพริกแกงแดง　　　1　ช้อนโต๊ะ
น้ำพริกเผา　　　　1　ช้อนโต๊ะ
น้ำตาล　　　　　1　ช้อนโต๊ะ
กะทิสดหรือครีม　　　2　ถ้วย
น้ำมะนาว　　　　1　ช้อนชา
เกลือ　　　　　1　ช้อนชา
ถั่วลิสงบ่นหรือเนยถั่ว　2　ช้อนโต๊ะ

วิธีทำ

เคี่ยวกะทิให้แตกมัน ช้อนกะทิ 2 ช้อน
โต๊ะใส่กะทะใช้ไฟอ่อน ๆ ผัดน้ำพริกทั้ง
สองอย่างจนหอม เติมกะทิทั้งหมดลงใน
กะทะใส่น้ำตาล เกลือ เนยถั่วคนให้เข้า
กันดีเติมน้ำมะนาว ชิมดูตามชอบยกลง

2 tablespoons powdered caraway
　and/or coriander seeds
1 teaspoon chopped lemon grass
1 teaspoon salt
1 teaspoon cinnamon
$\frac{1}{2}$ teaspoon cloves
2 tablespoons chopped red
　onion　(shallot)
5 cloves garlic
5 seeds of cardamom
1 teaspoon kapi (shrimp paste)
5 bay leaves
2 tablespoons vegetable oil

METHOD:

Brown garlic and red onion and
set aside. Remove seeds from chilies, drain the pods and chop fine.
Place in pan together with the other
spices. Cook over low heat until
brown. Pound to paste. Add salt,
the brown red onion and garlic and
last of all kapi. Heat the fry pan
with 2 tablespoons oil. Fry the paste
for 3 minutes, add 5 seeds of cardamom and 5 bay leaves. Cool.
Keeps well in tightly closed jar.

SATAY SAUCE

INGREDIENTS:

1 tablespoon red curry paste
　(see page 13)
1 tablespoon roasted curry paste
　(see page 11)
1 tablespoon sugar
2 tablespoons peanut butter

2 cups coconut milk or light
　cream
1 teaspoon lemon juice or
　tamarind juice
1 teaspoon salt

น้ำซ๊อสเปรี้ยวหวาน

ส่วน

น้ำตาล	1 ถ้วย
น้ำส้ม	$\frac{1}{4}$ ถ้วย
เกลือ	1 ช้อนชา
น้ำ	$\frac{1}{2}$ ถ้วย
ซ๊อสมะเขือเทศ	1 ช้อนโต๊ะ
แบ้งข้าวโพดละลายน้ำ	2 ช้อนโต๊ะ

วิธีทำ

เคี่ยวน้ำตาล เกลือ น้ำส้ม น้ำ จนเดือด ช้อนฟองทิ้ง ใส่ซ๊อสมะเขือเทศคนจน ละลาย ลดไฟ เติมแบ้งคนอย่าให้แบ้ง เบ็นลูก ทิ้งไว้จนเย็น ใส่ขวดบิดฝาไว้ ใช้ทำผัดเปรี้ยวหวาน จิ้มเกี๊ยวทอดและ ถ้าไม่ใส่แบ้งใช้ทำก๋วยเตี๋ยวผัดไทยก็ได้

อาจาด

ส่วน

น้ำตาล	2 ช้อนโต๊ะ
น้ำส้ม	1 ช้อนโต๊ะ
เกลือ	$\frac{1}{4}$ ช้อนชา
น้ำร้อน	2 ช้อนโต๊ะ
แตงกวาหั่น	1 ถ้วย
หัวหอมแดงฝาน	1 หัว
พริกแดงหั่น	1 เม็ด

วิธีทำ

ซงน้ำตาลเกลือด้วยน้ำร้อน พอละลาย เติมน้ำส้มทิ้งไว้ให้เย็น แตงกวาปอก เปลือกหั่นเบ็นชิ้นใส่ถ้วยฝานหอมแดงไว้

16

METHOD:

Heat the coconut milk until boiling. Add the 2 kinds of curry pastes and stir—fry. Add peanut butter, sugar, salt and lemon or tamarind juice.

SWEET AND SOUR SAUCE

INGREDIENTS:

- 1 cup sugar
- $\frac{1}{4}$ cup vinegar
- 1 teaspoon salt
- $\frac{1}{2}$ cup water
- 1 tablespoon Ketchup
- 2 tablespoons cornstarch mixed with water

METHOD:

In a small pot put the water, sugar, salt and vinegar. Using low heat, bring slowly to a boil. Add ketchup and stir. Add cornstarch gradually, stirring until it thickens. Remove from heat; cool. Put in a jar and cover. Use for sweet and sour sauce or as sauce for fried wanton. Without the cornstarch, may be used for Thai fried noodles.

CUCUMBER SALAD

INGREDIENTS:

- 2 tablespoons sugar
- 1 tablespoon vinegar
- $\frac{1}{4}$ teaspoon salt
- 2 tablespoons hot water
- 1 cup cucumber peeled and sliced
- 1 small red onion sliced thin
- 1 red chili pepper sliced

METHOD:

In a serving bowl, arrange cucumber; red onion and red chili pepper

บนวางพริกแดงลงบนหอม เทน้ำส้มผสม
ลงบนผักรับประทานกับแกงกะหรี่ ขนม
บึงหน้าหมู สะเต๊ะ เป็นต้น.

น้ำเชื่อม

ส่วน

น้ำตาล	3	ถ้วย
น้ำดอกมะลิ หรือ กลีบกุหลาบ	1	ถ้วย

วิธีทำ

ละลายน้ำตาลกับน้ำ ตั้งไฟจนเดือด
เคี่ยวต่อไป 15 นาที กรองด้วยผ้าขาวบาง
ทิ้งไว้จนเย็นลอยด้วยดอกมะลิ หรือกลีบ
กุหลาบ ใช้ทำลอยแก้ว พั้น หรือผสมกับ
น้ากะทิสด

ไข่กรอกหั้น

ส่วน

ไข่	3	ฟอง
เกลือ	$\frac{1}{4}$	ช้อนชา
น้ำมัน	1	ช้อนโต๊ะ

วิธีทำ

ทากะทะให้ทั่วด้วยน้ำมัน ตีไข่แบบทำไข่
เจียวเทลงในกะทะเพียงครึ่งหนึ่ง กรอก
ไปจนทั่ว พอไข่สุกตักออกทานน้ำมันอีก
กรอกส่วนที่สองเช่นเดียวกันตักขึ้นม้วน
แล้วหั่นเป็นเส้นเล็ก ๆ ใช้โรยหน้าข้าว
ผัด หมี่กะทิ เป็นต้น

หมายเหตุ ใช้ทำขนมแบ่งสิบชาววังต้อง
หั่นเป็นสี่เหลี่ยมเล็กๆ

---

in layers.
Mix the vinegar, sugar, salt, and
hot water until the sugar dissolved.
Pour over the cucumbers. Serve.

SUGAR SYRUP
(Nam chuam)

INGREDIENTS :

3 cups sugar
1 cup water
Jasmine flowers or rose petals

METHOD :

In a large pot, dissolve sugar and
water ; boil for 15 minutes or until
the syrup is formed. If necessary,
strain through cheescloth. Cool. Float
in jasmine flowers or rose petals.

FRIED EGG LIKE AN OMELET
(Khai Grog Hun)

INGREDIENTS:

3 eggs
$\frac{1}{4}$ teaspoon salt
1 tablespoon vegetable oil

METHOD:

Beat the eggs uniformly with fork.
Rub oil in clean frying pan with
paper towel. Heat, pour egg into
center of pan and quickly roll around
so it covers bottom of pan in a thin
layer. Cook over low heat until
egg is done. (about 1 minute), Remove egg and cut into small strips.

NOTE:

For steamed rice tarts with fish
filling (Kanom Jeep) cut into small
dice.

Side Dishes

๑. เนื้อเค็ม

ส่วน

เนื้อสำหรับอบ 1 ก้อน 3 ปอนด์ (1½ กิโล)
เกลือ 1 ช้อนโต๊ะ   น้ำปลา 2 ช้อนโต๊ะ
พริกไทย ½ ช้อนชา ผงชูรส 1 ช้อนชา
น้ำมันสำหรับทอด 2 ถ้วย กระดาษเช็ดมือ

วิธีทำ

แล่เนื้อเป็นชิ้นบาง ๆ   หนาประมาณ 1
กะเบียด   ติดมันบ้างก็ดี   เคล้าเกลือ
น้ำปลา ผงชูรสพริกไทย   หมักไว้ 2 ชม.
ตั้งกะทะแบน ๆ บนเตาไฟกลาง ๆ   แผ่

DRIED SALTY BEEF

INGREDIENTS:

    3 pound roast beef meat
    1 tablespoon salt
    2 tablespoon nampla (fish sauce)
    2 teaspoons MSG.
    ½ teaspoon pepper
    2 cups vegetable oil
    Paper towels

METHOD:

Slice the beef thin (do not cut off the fat). In a large bowl marinate the sliced beef with salt, nampla, pepper and MSG. for 2 hours.   In a saucepan lay the sliced beef and cook over medium heat for 3 min-

18

เนื้อลงในกะทะให้ทั่ว พอสุกกลับอีก
ข้าง (ประมาณข้างละ 2 นาที) ตักใส่
กระดาษซับน้ำให้แห้งจนหมดนำไปทอด
ในน้ำมันร้อนจัดต้องใช้น้ำมันมากๆ จะ
ได้เนื้อเค็มที่อร่อย และไม่ต้องตากแดด
หรืออบเลย

2. ไข่เค็ม

ส่วน

เกลือ ¾ ถ้วย น้ำ 4 ถ้วย ไข่ 12 ฟอง

วิธีทำ

ต้มเกลือจนเดือดทิ้งไว้จนอุ่นจัดๆ เรียง
ไข่ ลงในขวดโหล เทน้ำเกลือให้ท่วม
ไข่ปิดฝาทิ้งไว้ประมาณ 30 หรือ 45 วัน
ตักไข่มาต้มจนสุก

หมายเหตุ ถ้าใช้ไข่ไก่ ไข่ขาวจะไม่
ค่อยแข็งมากแต่ไข่แดงจะแดงดีและแข็ง

หมูหวาน

ส่วน

หมูหั่น 1 ถ้วย หัวหอมหั่นเป็นเส้น
¾ ถ้วย น้ำตาลทรายขาว 2 ช้อนโต๊ะ
น้ำตาลสีรำ 1 ช้อนโต๊ะ น้ำปลา 2 ช้อน
โต๊ะ น้ำมัน 2 ช้อนโต๊ะ แป้งสาลี 1 ช้อนชา

วิธีทำ

ตั้งกะทะใส่น้ำมันจนร้อน ใส่แป้งสาลี
พอละลายใส่หอมหั่น ตามด้วยหมูผัดจน
สุก ใส่น้ำตาลทั้งสองอย่าง ใส่น้ำปลา
ผัดต่อไปจนเข้าเนื้อกันดีแล้วตักใส่จาน
หรือจะทำทีละมากๆ ใส่ขวดปิดฝาเข้า
ตู้เย็นไว้ก็ได้ เวลาจะใช้ก็นำมาอุ่น

utes on each side. Drain thoroughly
on paper towels. Fry the beef in
deep hot oil until brown. Remove
from fat and drain. Serve as side
dish with curry or as hors d' oeuvre.

SALTY EGG
(Khai Kem)

INGREDIENTS:
   3/4 cup salt
   4 quarts water
   12 eggs (Duck eggs may be
   used)

METHOD:
Add salt to water and bring to boil.
Remove from heat; Cool to luke-
warm.

Arrange the eggs in a big jar or
crock; Pour over the lukewarm boiled
salt water. Cover and let stand for
30—45 days. Before use, hard boil
the salty egg. Use to garnish food.

SWEET PORK
(Moo Warn)

INGREDIENTS:
   1 cup pork cut into small pieces
   $\frac{1}{4}$ cup chopped onion
   2 tablespoons sugar
   1 tablespoon light brown sugar
   2 tablespoons nampla   (Fish
   sauce)
   2 tablespoons vegetable oil
   1 teaspoon flour

METHOD:
In fry pan brown the flour; add
pork, onion and stir well. Cook until
the pork is done. Season with sugar,
brown sugar, nampla and stir—fry
until the gravy is thick. Spoon into
a serving dish. Serve with purple
fried rice, Namprik long rua. (Can
be cooked ahead of time and kept
in the refrigerator)

Pineapple Punch

The following nine pages contain suggestions on how to produce a balanced Thai meal, starting with Pineapple Punch and ending up with Custard. You should understand that Thai meals are usually eaten in a group with three or more main dishes of different tastes (sweet, salty, hot and sour, neutral, etc.), neutralized by steamed rice which is always the staple part of a Thai meal. Each diner may eat only those dishes he prefers, not necessarily every dish. But you should try all of them first before you decide, right?

พั้นสับปะรด

ส่วน

สับปะรด ขนาดย่อม	8	ผล
น้ามะนาวคั้น	$\frac{1}{2}$	ถ้วย
น้าเชอรี่	$\frac{1}{4}$	ถ้วย
น้าตาล	1	ปอนด์
น้า	1	ถ้วย
น้าร้อน	1	ถ้วย
เหล้ารัม	2	เป๊ก
เหล้าแม่โขง	2	เป๊ก
เหล้ายิน	2	เป๊ก
ใบสะระแหน่	8	กิ่ง
ดอกแวนด้า	8	ดอก
ลูกเชอรี่	8	ลูก
ส้มหั่นเป็นชิ้น ๆ	8	ชิ้น
น้าแข็ง		

วิธีทำ

ต้มน้ำตาลกับน้ำ 1 ถ้วย พอเดือด
กรองด้วยผ้าขาวบาง พักไว้ ตัดสับปะ
รดต่ำลงมาจากหน่อประมาณ 2 นิ้ว ตัด
ก้านออก ใช้พิมพ์สำหรับชักไส้ดึงเนื้อ
สับปะรด ออกมาจนหมดทั้ง 8 ผลนำเนื้อ
สับปะรด มาสับฝานจนชิดไส้ เติมน้ำ
ร้อน 1 ถ้วย คั้นแบบคั้นกะทิกรองด้วย
กระชอน ผสมน้ำสับปะรด กับน้ำมะ-
นาว น้ำเชื่อม น้ำเชอรี่ เหล้าทั้งสาม
อย่าง คนให้เข้ากันดี ใส่น้ำแข็งให้เต็ม
ลูก สับปะรดเทส่วนผสมพื้นลงไป แต่ง
ด้วยเชอรี่ (ลูกเชอรี่ซึ่งเสียบไว้กับส้ม)
ใบสะระแหน่ 1 กิ่ง และดอกแวนด้า 1
ดอก เสริฟ

PINEAPPLE PUNCH

INGREDIENTS:

- 8 medium pineapples
- $\frac{1}{2}$ cup lemon juice or lime juice
- $\frac{1}{4}$ cup Maraschino cherry juice
- 3 cups sugar
- 1 cup water
- 1 cup hot water
- 2 jiggers Jamaica Rum
- 2 jiggers Dry Gin
- 2 jiggers Mae Khong Thai Whisky or Borbon
- 8 sprigs mint
- 8 vanda Orchids (optional)
- 8 maraschino cherries
- 1 orange cut into 8 wedges
- 4 pound ice cubes

METHOD:

Boil 1 cup water and sugar until thick syrup is formed. (about 10 to 15 minutes). Strain (if necessary) set aside to cool. Using a pineapple cutter, cut each pineapple into a shape of a bowl. Chop pineapple meat into fine pieces, pour over hot water, squeeze pineapple juice, and strain.

Combine in punch bowl: pineapple juice, lemon juice, Maraschino juice, cooked syrup, Rum, and Whisky. Stir slightly. Fill pineapple bowls (or glasses) with ice cubes; spoon the punch mixture over and garnish with sprig of mint, maraschino cherry, orange wedge and Vanda orchid. Makes 8 or more servings.

21

Steamed rice tarts
with fish filling

When Her Majesty Queen Elizabeth II of
England and The Duke of Edinburgh visited Thailand
a few years ago, the House of Kunjara set up an
exhibition of Thai Food prepared at a small Thai
house in the Ancient City, South of Bangkok. I
took part in making this dish which was later
served at tea. Both Their Majesties the King and
Queen of Thailand were their hosts at this function.

ขนมจีบปั้นสิบชาววัง (ไส้ปลา)

ส่วน

แบ่งข้าวเจ้า	2	ถ้วย
แบ่งท้าวยายม่อม	1	ช้อนโต๊ะ
แบ่งมัน (ใช้เวลาปั้น)	1	ถ้วย
น้ำ	2	ถ้วย
ปลาเนื้อล้วนนึ่งแล้วยี		
(กะพงขาว, ซามอนด์)	1	ถ้วย
หัวหอมแดงสับละเอียด	$\frac{1}{2}$	ถ้วย
พริกไทยบ่น	$\frac{1}{2}$	ช้อนชา
หอมขาวสับละเอียด	$\frac{1}{2}$	ถ้วย
กระเทียมสับละเอียด	1	ช้อนชา
ก้านผักชีสับละเอียด	1	ช้อนชา
ใบผักชีหั่นละเอียด	1	ช้อนโต๊ะ
เกลือ	1	ช้อนชา
น้ำตาล	1	ช้อนโต๊ะ
น้ำปลา	1	ช้อนชา

ไข่ไก่ 3 ฟองกรอกหั่นเป็นสี่เหลี่ยมเล็กๆ

น้ำมัน	1	ถ้วย

ผักกาดหอม   ผักชี   พริกสด

วิธีทำ

ละลายแบ่งทั้งสองอย่างในหม้อก้นลึกใช้ มอบแบ่งจนไม่เป็นเม็ด ตั้งไฟกวนด้วย พายไม้จนสุก นำมายีในจานด้วยช้อนจน ไม่เป็นลูก ใช้มือชุบน้ำนวดแบ่งจน เหนียวดีแล้ว แตะแบ่งมันทำเป็นก้อน ยาวๆใส่ชามปิดฝาครอบไว้

ใช้น้ำมันทากะทะ กรอกไข่ให้บางที่ สุด (แบบทำไข่ยัดไส้) แล้วม้วนหั่นเป็น

STEAMED RICE TARTS WITH FISH FILLING

INGREDIENTS :

- 2 cups rice flour
- 1 tablespoon starch (pang taw yai mom) (if cornstarch is substituted. use 2 tablespoons)
- 1 cup cornstarch (use while shaping)
- 1 quart water
- 1 cup fish meat steamed and minced
- $\frac{1}{2}$ cup minced red onion
- $\frac{1}{2}$ cup minced white onion
- $\frac{1}{2}$ teaspoon pepper
- 1 teaspoon minced garlic
- 1 teaspoon minced coriander stalks
- 1 teaspoon chopped fine corian der leaves
- 1 teaspoon salt
- 1 teaspoon sugar
- 1 teaspoon nampla (fish sauce)
- 3 eggs made into omelet and chopped
- 1 cup vegetable oil lettuce, coriander, chili

METHOD:

COMBINE: Rice flour, starch and water in a large pot: bring to boil and cook, stirring constantly, until mixture coats a spoon. Remove from heat, and turn onto a large plate. Knead until smooth and elastic, (moistening hands in water as necessary). Divide dough and shape into approximately ten sticks, roll in cornstarch, put into a bowl and cover. Set aside.

Steps in making steamed rice tart

There are two ways to make the tart, the ordinary way and the "Khanom Jeeb" way, both methods are illustrated below.

We start with the flour in a ball. We flatten the ball into a half cup and fill it with the fish filling, then we make a choice.

We can fold the cup edge together and make a half circle tart. Close the half circle edge like fluted edge in making pie. It is then ready to be steamed. The harder way is to fold the cup rim into a taller cup with many fine folds and press them together into a pointed top. The last step is to flatten the top a little as shown in the picture. The final product is called "Khanom Jeeb" in Thai meaning folded tidbit.

You must try to make it without rupturing the skin. Do not feel bad if you can not do the "Khanom Jeeb" the first time. After all my experience, I can only fold "eight" perfect "Khanom Jeebs" in <u>one</u> hour. The tart is much easier to make.

สี่เหลี่ยมเล็ก ๆ พักไว้

ผัดไส้ใช้น้ำมัน 2 ช้อนโต๊ะ เจียวกระ-
เทียมกับก้านผักชีสับพอเหลือง ใส่ปลา
(นึ่งพอสุกนำมายีด้วยซ่อม) หอมสับทั้ง
สองอย่าง ผัดต่อไปจนเข้ากันดี ใส่เกลือ
พริกไทย   น้ำปลา   น้ำตาล   ผัดต่อไป
ใส่ไข่กรอกหั่นละเอียดและใบผักชีคนให้
เข้ากัน ยกลง   แบ่งแบ่งเป็นก้อนกลม
เส้นผ่าศูนย์กลาง1นิ้ว ใช้แบ่งมันทานิ้ว
มืออย่าให้แบ่งติดมือ แผ่เป็นรูปกะทะตัก
ไส้ใส่ตรงกลางบีบปลายให้ติดกันพับจีบ
สำหรับขนมจีบเมื่อคลี่แบ่งเป็นรูปกะทะ
แล้ว   ใช้นิ้วหัวแม่มือและนิ้วชี้จับเป็น
จีบรอบ ๆ เทไส้ลงตรงกลาง   รอบปาก
ทำเป็นหวนก   เมื่อจีบจบหมดแบ่ง
และไส้แล้วเรียงใส่ลังถึงรองด้วยใบตอง
(หรือกระดาษตะกั่ว)   เจาะรูเล็ก ๆ พอ
ให้ไอน้ำรอดขึ้นมาได้   ทาน้ำมันบนใบ
ตองก่อน   นึ่งขณะน้ำเดือดจัดชุดละ 3
นาทียกลงเรียงใส่จานพรมด้วยน้ำมัน รับ
ประทานกับผักชี ผักกาดหอม พริกสด

Brown the minced garlic and minced
coriander stalk in a heavy skillet
until golden brown.   Add onions
and fish stirring constantly.   Add
salt, pepper sugar, nampla and
toss lightly. Add chopped egg and
chopped coriander leaves.   Mix.
Remove from heat.   Spoon into a
bowl.

Shape the dough into small balls
(8 to 10 per stick) Shape each ball
into a small cup; (see picture) fill
with fish filling; fold over like a
tart. Arrange the tarts in steamer
(lined with alumium foil which has
been pricked with a fork); steam
for 3 minutes.   Sprinkle with oil
arrange on serving plate, garnish
with lettuce, coriander and chili.

*สำหรับขนมจีบนี้   ผู้เขียนเคยบันถวาย
สมเด็จพระราชินีอังกฤษ   พระนางเจ้า
เอลิซาเบธที่สองและพระสวามี   ที่วัง
โบราณ คราวเสด็จเมืองไทยเป็นทางการ
และขึ้นถวายเจ้าฟ้าหญิงสิรินทรฯ เมื่อ
วันประสูติ ปี 2516 ณ. วังจิตรลดา*

Pork curry country style

แกงป่าหมู

ส่วน

หมูติดมันหั่นเป็นชิ้นเล็กๆ	1 ถ้วย
น้ำพริกแกงแดง	3 ช้อนโต๊ะ
เห็ดแชมเปญสดผ่าสอง	1 ถ้วย
กะหล่ำปลีหั่นเป็นสี่เหลี่ยม	½ ถ้วย
ถั่วแขกหั่นเป็นท่อนๆ ละ 1 ½ นิ้ว	
	½ ถ้วย
พริกหยวกสีแดงหั่นเส้นๆ	½ ถ้วย

PORK CURRY COUNTRY STYLE

INGREDIENTS:

1 cup pork sliced into 2 inch strips

3 tablespoons red curry paste (see page 13)

1 cup fresh mushrooms cut in halves

½ cup chopped cabbage

½ cup green beans cut into 1½ inch segments

น้ำปลา	2 ช้อนโต๊ะ
น้ำตาลทราย	1 ช้อนชา
กะชายแห้ง (แช่น้ำอุ่น)	1 ช้อนโต๊ะ
	(ถ้าชอบ)
ใบสะระแหน่	10 ใบ
น้ำมันพืช	$\frac{1}{2}$ ถ้วย

วิธีทำ

หั่นผักทั้งสามอย่างแช่น้ำเย็นไว้ ตั้งกะทะ
ใส่น้ำมันพอน้ำมันร้อนใส่เครื่องแกงแดง
ผัดจนหอมใส่หมูเติมน้ำปลาผัดต่อไปจน
สุก หยิบผักทั้งหมดขึ้นจากน้ำใส่ลงใน
กะทะพอสุกใส่กระชายใบสะระแหน่ และ
พริกหยวกผัดเบาๆ จนเข้ากันดีตักใส่
ชามเสริฟ

หมายเหตุ ถ้าชอบมีน้ำมากๆเติมน้ำสุก
สัก $\frac{1}{2}$ ถ้วยพอเดือดยกลง

น่องไก่ทอด

ส่วน

น่องไก่	8 น่อง
ผงกระเทียมเกลือ	1 ช้อนชา
ซีอิ๊วญี่ปุ่น (คิโคแมน)	1 ช้อนโต๊ะ
พริกไทย	$\frac{1}{2}$ ช้อนชา
น้ำมัน	1 ช้อนโต๊ะ
แป้งสาลี	$\frac{1}{2}$ ถ้วย
น้ำมันสำหรับทอด	2 ถ้วย
ต้นหอมหั่น	1 ต้น

$\frac{1}{2}$ cup red chili cut into strips

2 tablespoons nampla (fish sauce)

1 teaspoon sugar

1 tablespoon Krachai (see glossary) optional

10 mint leaves

$\frac{1}{2}$ cup vegetable oil

METHOD:

Soak cut vegetables in cold water for 15 minutes. In a large frying pan heat the oil, stir in red curry paste. Add pork and nampla and stir—fry for 5 minutes. Lift vegetables from water and quickly add to pan. Stir—fry about 3 minutes. Sprinkle with sugar and toss lightly. Spoon to a serving bowl. Garnish with mint leaves. Serve hot.

FRIED CHICKEN DRUMSTICKS

INGREDIENTS:

8 chicken drumsticks

1 teaspoon garlic salt

1 tablespoon soy sauce

$\frac{1}{2}$ teaspoon pepper

1 tablespoon vegetable oil

$\frac{1}{2}$ cup flour

2 cups vegetable oil

1 tablespoon spring onion coarsely chopped

METHOD:

Marinate the drumsticks with garlic salt, Pepper, and soy sauce and 1 tablespoon oil for 2 hours. Roll drumsticks in flour Deep — fry drumsticks 4 at a time in hot oil for $3\frac{1}{2}$ minutes. Drain thoroughly on paper towel. Arrange on serving plate. Garnish with spring onion.

วิธีทำ

หมักน่องไก่ด้วยผงกระเทียม เกลือ พริก
ไทย ซีอิ๊วญี่ปุ่นน้ำมันทิ้งไว้สัก 2 ชม.
ก่อนทอดเคล้าลงในแบ๋งสาลีจนทั่ว ทอด
ในน้ำมันร้อนจัดจนเหลืองอ่อน ลดไฟ
ทอดต่อไปจนเกรียม ตักขึ้นวางบนกระ-
ดาษซับน้ำมันทอดต่อไปจนหมด จัดใส่
จานเวลาเสริฟโรยด้วยต้นหอมหั่น

ผัดแอสปารากัสกับไส้กรอก

ส่วน

ไส้กรอกค็อกเทล	16	อัน
แอสปารากัสหั่น	2	ถ้วย
ผงกระเทียมเกลือ	1	ช้อนชา
น้ำมัน	3	ช้อนโต๊ะ
น้ำปลา	1	ช้อนชา

วิธีทำ

ไส้กรอกผ่าสี่ทั้งหัวท้าย หั่นแอสปารากัส
เป็นท่อนๆละ 1 $\frac{1}{2}$ นิ้วแช่น้ำเย็น ตั้งกะ
ทะใส่น้ำมันพอร้อนจัดใส่ไส้กรอกพอสุก
หยิกผักขึ้นจากน้ำใส่ลงในกะทะ โรย
ด้วยเกลือกระเทียม ผัดพอสุกอย่าให้สุก
มาก ใส่น้ำปลาตักใส่ชาม

ต้มยำกุ้ง

ส่วน

กุ้งสด 10 ตัว	เห็ดกระดุมกระป๋อง	1
ถ้วย	ตะไคร้ (ตัดเป็นท่อนๆ) 1 ต้น	

28

FRIED ASPARAGUS WITH SAUSAGES

INGREDIENTS:

    16 cocktail sausages
    1 cup asparagus cut in 2 inch
       segments
    1 teaspoon garlic salt
    3 tablespoons vegetable oil
    1 teaspoon nampla (fish sauce)

METHOD:

Cut both ends of sausages in
fourths so that they look like
flowers. Soak the cleaned, cut
asparagus in cold water for 10
minutes.

Heat 3 tablespoons oil in large
frying pan. Add sausages, tossing
lightly for 2 minutes add asparagus
and stir—fry for another 2 minutes.
Sprinkle with garlic salt and nampla; turn. Spoon onto serving plate.
Serve.

SOUR SHRIMP SOUP
(Tom yum goong)

INGREDIENTS:

    10 medium shrimp
    1 cup button mushrooms
                 (canned)
    1 stalk lemon grass or 2 pieces
      lemon peel
    2 magrood leaves(see glossary)
      optional
    $\frac{1}{2}$ teaspoon salt
    $\frac{1}{2}$ teaspoon MSG,
    2 tablespoons nampla
                (fish sauce)
    2 tablespoons lemon or lime
      juice
    $\frac{1}{2}$ teaspoon chili powder

ใบมะกรูด 2 ใบ เกลือ $\frac{1}{2}$ ช้อนชา ผงชู
รส $\frac{1}{2}$ ช้อนชา น้ำปลา 2 ช้อนโต๊ะ น้ำ
มะนาว 2 ช้อนโต๊ะ พริกป่น $\frac{1}{2}$ ช้อนชา
ผักชี 1 ต้น น้ำ 2 ถ้วย

วิธีทำ

กุ้งสดปอกผ่าหลังชักเส้นดำล้างผึ่งไว้ ต้ม
น้ำพอเดือด ใส่ใบมะกรูด ตะไคร้ กุ้ง
พอกุ้งสุก ใส่เห็ดใส่เกลือผงชูรสเทใส่
ชาม เติมน้ำปลา มะนาวพริกป่น ชิม
ดูตามชอบ ตักใส่ถ้วยเสริฟทั้ง 8 ใบโรย
ด้วยผักชีเสริฟร้อน ๆ

ขนมหม้อแกงเมืองเพชร

ส่วน

น้ำกะทิหวาน	1 ถ้วย
ไข่	5 ฟอง
น้ำตาลอ้อย	$\frac{1}{2}$ ถ้วย
น้ำตาลทราย	$\frac{1}{2}$ ถ้วย
ครีม	2 ช้อนโต๊ะ

วิธีทำ

น้ำกะทิหวานใช้มะพร้าว 2 กระป๋อง
(Angle Flake Coconut) ใส่น้ำร้อน
1 ถ้วย คั้นน้ำจะได้น้ำกะทิหวาน 1 ถ้วย
ตีไข่กับน้ำตาลทรายทั้งสองอย่างเติมน้ำ
กะทิหวานและครีม ตั้งไฟอ่อนๆหมั่นคน
เสมอ ๆ จนสุกเทใส่ถาดอบด้วยไฟ 350°
ประมาณ 30 นาทีพอแห้ง เอาอบไว้ใต้
เตาจนหน้าเกรียมเอาออกจากเตาอบทั้ง
ไว้ให้เย็น ตัดได้ 8 ชิ้น

8 sprigs coriander
1 quart water

METHOD:

Wash, peel and cut shrimp. Bring
the water to boil, add lemon grass
(lemon peel) and Magrood leaves.
Drop in shrimp and simmer gently
for 3 minutes. Add mushrooms,
salt and MSG. Remove from heat,
season with nampla, lemon juice,
and chili powder. Spoon into individual serving dishes. Garnish with
sprigs of coriander. Serve hot.

CUSTARD
(Kanom Mokang Muang Petch)

INGREDIENTS:

- 1 cup sweet coconut milk (see glossary)
- 5 eggs well beaten
- $\frac{1}{2}$ cup light brown sugar
- $\frac{1}{2}$ cup sugar
- 2 tablespoons light cream

METHOD:

For sweet coconut milk use 7 or 8
ounces (2 cans) Angel Flake
coconut, add 1 cup hot water, squeeze to get coconut milk.

Preheat oven to 350 degrees.

Combine: Coconut milk, cream,
brown sugar, sugar and well beaten egg. Pour into a large pot
and cook over medium heat approximately 10 minutes until done
(It will be like very soft scrambled
eggs).

Pour slowly into 9 inch square pan
and bake about 30 minutes. Remove from the oven. Place under
broiler and broil until golden brown.
Cool. Cut into small pieces.

Turkey rice soup

For breakfast, the Thai prefers rice soup to regular egg dishes customary in American Homes. The following two dishes are also popular as snacks or suppers. They are so easy to make, if you are a student or housewife in a hurry, you could even use cooked minute rice to replace regularly cooked rice and save a little time.

ข้าวต้มไก่งวง

ส่วน

ไก่งวงกระป๋อง	1 กระป๋อง
น้ำ	3 ถ้วย
ข้าวสุก	1 ถ้วยครึ่ง
หัวหอมหั่นเป็นวงครึ่งวงแหวน1หัวย่อมๆ	
ต้นหอมกับเซลเลอรี่หั่นฝอย 1 ช้อนโต๊ะ	
น้ำปลา	1 ช้อนโต๊ะ
น้ำมันพืช	2 ช้อนโต๊ะ
ขนมปังหั่นเป็น4เหลี่ยมลูกเต๋า2ช้อนโต๊ะ	
พริกไทย	$\frac{1}{4}$ ช้อนชา

วิธีทำ

ตั้งกะทะไฟอ่อนๆ ใช้น้ำมัน 2 ช้อนโต๊ะ ทอดขนมปังจนเหลืองกรอบตักใส่กระ – ดาษซับน้ำมันพักไว้

เปิดไก่งวงกระป๋อง ผสมน้ำตั้งไฟจน เดือดใส่หัวหอมน้ำปลา พริกไทยเติม ข้าวเคี่ยวต่อไปสัก 10 นาที ตักใส่ชาม โรย ด้วยต้มหอมกับใบเซลเลอรี่หั่นฝอย และขนมปังกรอบ เสิร์ฟร้อนๆ เป็น อาหารเช้าหรืออาหารว่าง

TURKEY RICE SOUP

INGREDIENTS:
- 1 can of turkey (small)
- 3 cups of water
- 1$\frac{1}{2}$ cups of cooked rice
- 1 whole onion cut in small pieces (half onion ring)
- 1 tablespoon chopped green onions and celery leaves
- 1 tablespoon nampla (fish sauce)
- $\frac{1}{2}$ teaspoon pepper

METHOD:
Place turkey in medium sized pot. Add 3 cups of water. Bring to boil. Add cooked steam rice, onion, nampla, and pepper. Cook for ten minutes. Put in serving bowl (or small soup bowl) top it with green vegetables. Serve hot. Makes two to three servings.

Chicken rice soup

When my husband was a young student at West Nottingham Academy in Maryland 22 years ago, he used to cook chicken rice soup in his dormitory. He cooked it at night after "light out" or during the weekend morning. He only used canned chicken, Minute rice and water.

My recipe calls for a little more effort. But if you are in a hurry, you may use canned chicken and skip the part of making chicken broth.

โจ๊ก

RICE SOUP

ส่วน

ข้าวใหม่	1	ถ้วย
น้ำ	3	ถ้วย
หมูบดหรือเนื้อไก่บด	½	ถ้วย
ขิงหั่นฝอย	1	ช้อนโต๊ะ
น้ำปลา	2	ช้อนโต๊ะ
พริกไทย	¼	ช้อนชา
ผักชีต้นหอมหั่นละเอียด	1	ช้อนโต๊ะ
ไข่	2	ฟอง

ผงชูรสชนิดหน่อย

กระดูกไก่ หรือ กระดูกหมู น้ำ 2 ถ้วย

วิธีทำ

ซาวข้าวให้สะอาด เติมน้ำ 3 ถ้วย เคี่ยว
ประมาณ 45 นาที หรือ 1 ชม. จนข้าว
เละ นำมาใส่กระชอนบดให้ละเอียด
ต้มน้ำกับกระดูกไก่ หรือกระดูกหมู
กรองเอาแต่น้ำให้ได้สัก 2 ถ้วยเทลงผสม
กับข้าวบดตั้งให้เดือดเติมไก่ หรือหมูบด
(ถ้าหมูบดปั้นเป็นก้อน ๆ แล้วค่อย ๆ
หยอดลงในข้าวกำลังเดือด) เติมน้ำปลา
ต่อยไข่ไก่ ใส่ชาม ชามละใบตักโจ๊กลง
ในชามโรยด้วย ขิงฝอยและผักชีต้น–
หอมโรยด้วยพริกไทย เสริฟร้อนๆเป็น
อาหารเช้าหรืออาหารว่างกลางคืน

INGREDIENTS :

- 1 cup rice
- 3 cups water
- ½ cup ground pork or sliced chic.
  ken meat
- 1 tablespoon chopped ginger
  root
- 2 tablespoons nampla (fish
  sauce)
- ¼ teaspoon pepper
- 1 tablespoon chopped green
  onion and coriander
- 2 eggs
  bones of chicken
- 2 cups water

METHOD :

Clean the rice well. Add 3 cups of
water in medium sized pot. Cook
for 45 minutes to 1 hour (low heat)
until the rice is soft. Remove from
heat. Pour into a double strainer.
Press with spoon until the rice becomes small pieces. Set aside.

Boil the chicken bones with 2 cups
of water. Cook them for 5 to 10
minutes. Remove bones. Add rice
to chicken broth. Cook for 2 minu
tes ; add ground pork or sliced chi·
cken little by little. Add nampla.

Break the eggs into the serving bowl.
Put the rice soup on top of the eggs.
Sprinkle with ginger, green onions
and chopped coriander. Makes 3-4
servings.

Chicken Satay

สะเต๊ะไก่

ส่วน

เนื้อไก่อกหั่นเป็นชิ้นยาวๆ ขนาดนิ้วก้อย
2 ถ้วย   ขิงสดหั่นหนาๆ 3 แว่น
กระเทียมกลีบงามๆ   3 กลีบ
ผงกะหรี่   1 ช้อนโต๊ะ
ลูกผักชียี่หร่าคั่วบ่น   1 ช้อนโต๊ะ
ครีม   3 ช้อนโต๊ะ
เกลือ   1 ช้อนชา
เนย   2 ช้อนโต๊ะ
หัวกะทิสด   ½ ถ้วย
ไม้สำหรับเสียบ

CHICKEN SATAY

INGREDIENTS :

(2 pounds) of chicken breasts,
cut in one inch strips knead
with the following ingredients,
adding one at time. Marinate
for at least two hours.
3 slices ginger (crushed)
3 cloves garlic (crushed)
1 tablespoon curry powder
1 tablespoon coriander powder

1 teaspoon salt
2 tablespoons butter

34

๙๕

นาจิ้ม

น้ำพริกแกงแดง	1	ช้อนโต๊ะ
น้ำพริกเผา	1	ช้อนโต๊ะ
น้ำตาล	1	ช้อนโต๊ะ
ถั่วลิสงบ่นหรือเนยถั่ว	2	ช้อนโต๊ะ
กะทิสดหรือครีม	$1\frac{1}{2}$	ถ้วย
น้ำมะนาว	1	ช้อนชา
เกลือ	1	ช้อนชา

วิธีทำนาจิ้ม

เคี่ยวกะทิให้แตกมัน   ช้อนกะทิสัก 2
ช้อนโต๊ะ   ใส่กะทะใช้ไฟอ่อนๆผัดน้ำ
พริกทั้งสองอย่างจนหอมเติมกะทิทั้งหมด
ลงในกะทะใส่น้ำตาล เกลือ เนยถั่ว คน
ให้เข้ากันดี เติมน้ำมะนาว ชิมดูตามชอบ

วิธีหมักเนื้อไก่

ตำขิงกับกระเทียมให้ละเอียดตักขึ้นพัก
ไว้ ใช้ชามก้นลึกเคล้าเนื้อไก่กับขิงและ
กระเทียมซึ่งเติมเกลือ   เครื่องเทศทุก
อย่างเคล้าให้เข้าเนื้อกันดี   ใส่นมและ
เนยใช้ซ้อมคนเบาๆ   หมักไว้อย่างน้อย
สองชั่วโมง

วิธีเสียบ

หลังจากหมักเนื้อไก่ได้ที่แล้ว เสียบเนื้อ
ไก่ไม้ละ 2 ชิ้นควรให้ติดกัน   ก่อนย่าง
ใช้หัวกะทิสดพรมให้ทั่ว   ย่างด้วยไฟ
ถ่านไม่ควรแรงมาก   เรียงใส่จานเสริฟ
กับน้ำจิ้มและอาจาด

3 tablespoons light cream
$\frac{1}{2}$ cup coconut milk
satay sticks

Thread a few pieces of chicken on
the top half of each satay stick.
Cook over charcoal. while cooking
sprinkle coconut milk on chicken.

SAUCE :

1 tablespoon red curry paste
(see page 13)
1 tablespoon roasted chili curry
paste (see page 11)
1 tablespoon sugar
2 tablespoons peanut butter
$1\frac{1}{2}$ cups of coconut milk or cream
1 tablespoon lemon juice or
tamarind juice
1 teaspoon salt

Heat the coconut milk until boiling.
Add the 2 kinds of curry paste and
stir fry. Add peanut butter, sugar,
salt and tamarind juice. (or lemon
juice)

The sauce should have a salty,
sweet and a little sour taste. Chicken satay makes an excellent hors
d'oeuvre. Serve with cucumber salad (see page16)

Tuna fish Salad

The Thai loves to drink and eat like Americans and others. The following dishes serve as appetizers or can be snacks or Small lunches in themselves.

เมี่ยงทูน่า

ส่วน

ปลาทูน่า	1	กระป๋อง
หมูบด	1	ถ้วย
ขิงหั่นฝอย	2	ช้อนโต๊ะ
หัวหอมแดงหั่น	2	ช้อนโต๊ะ
ผงกระเทียม	$\frac{1}{2}$	ช้อนชา
เกลือ	1	ช้อนชา
น้ำมะนาว	2	ช้อนโต๊ะ
ผิวมะนาวหั่น	$\frac{1}{2}$	ช้อนโต๊ะ
มะพร้าวคั่ว	2	ช้อนโต๊ะ
ผักกาดหอม ผักชี พริกบ่น		
ถั่วลิสงคั่ว	$\frac{1}{2}$	ถ้วย

วิธีทำ

รวนหมูบดในกะทะ ไม่ต้องใส่น้ำมัน พอหมูสุก เทใส่ชามใหญ่ เปิดปลาทูน่า กระป๋องบีบน้ำออก ผสมด้วยกันกับหมู เคล้าให้เข้ากัน ใส่ผงกระเทียมเกลือ มะนาว ชิมดูตามชอบ เติมขิงหั่นฝอย หัวหอม ผิวมะนาว จัดเป็นคำๆวางบน ใบผักกาดหอม โรยด้วย ถั่วลิสง มะ พร้าวคั่ว ผักชีและพริกบ่น เป็นกับ แกล้ม ได้อย่างดี

TUNA FISH SALAD

INGREDIENTS:

1 can chunk tuna fish (8 ozs.)
1 cup ground pork
2 tablespoons finely chopped ginger root
2 tablespoons chopped red on-ion
$\frac{1}{2}$ teaspoon garlic powder
1 teaspoon salt
2 tablespoons lime juice
$\frac{1}{2}$ tablespoon lime peel
2 tablespoons ground roasted coconut
$\frac{1}{2}$ cup peanuts
1 teaspoon chili powder
lettuce and coriander

METHOD:

Cook the ground pork in frying pan without oil for 3 minutes or until well cooked. Place in bowl. Drain the tuna fish and add to the cooked pork; mix well. Add garlic powder, salt, lime juice. Blend together. Add chopped ginger, chopped red onion, chopped lime peel. Decorate the plate with lettuce leaves. Spoon tuna mixture on individual lettuce leaves. Top with roasted coconut, peanuts, coriander leaves and chili powder. Serve as a finger food.

Hot shrimp Salad

Most Americans when they tried Thai Food, would comment on the very sharp taste of the dish. Thai food has strong taste because it is always taken with rice which neutralize much of the effect. Some famous dishes are eaten without rice, like this hot and sour shrimp salad. It goes well with beer or tall drinks before dinner. It is garanteed to wake up your taste bud, sometimes it even makes you forget dinner.

<table>
<tr><td>

พล่ากุ้ง

ส่วน

กุ้งปอกผ่าหลังทำสะอาด	1	ถ้วย
ตะไคร้หั่นฝอย	1	ช้อนโต๊ะ
หัวหอมแดงหั่น	1	ช้อนโต๊ะ
มะนาว	2	ช้อนโต๊ะ
น้ำปลา	1	ช้อนโต๊ะ
ผงเกลือกระเทียม	1	ช้อนชา
ต้นหอม ผักชี หั่นฝอย	1	ช้อนโต๊ะ
ใบสะระแหน่	10	ใบ
ผักกาดหอม	1	ต้น

วิธีทำ

ห่อกุ้งด้วยกระดาษตะกั่วย่างบนเตาแก๊ส
หรือเตาไฟฟ้าก็ได้ข้างละ 2 นาที พอกุ้ง
สุกแก้ห่อเทใส่ชาม ผสมด้วยมะนาว
น้ำปลา เกลือ กะเทียมผงเคล้าให้เข้า
กัน แล้วใส่ตะไคร้หั่นหอมแดงหั่น
และต้นหอมผักชีหั่นฝอย โรยหน้าด้วย
พริกป่นและใบสะระแหน่ จัดผักกาด
หอมไว้ข้าง ๆ

</td><td>

HOT AND SOUR SHRIMP SALAD

INGREDIENTS :

- 1 cup shelled and cleaned shrimp
- 1 tablespoon finely chopped lemon grass (see glossary)
- 1 tablespoon sliced red onion
- 1 tablespoon nampla (fish sauce)
- 2 tablespoons lemon or lime juice
- 1 teaspoon garlic salt
- 1 teaspoon chili powder
- 1 tablespoon chopped spring onion and coriander
- 10 mint leaves
- 1 lettuce

METHOD :

Using aluminum foil, wrap the shrimp. Place on the burner and cook for 2 minutes on each side. Unwrap and place in a bowl. Season with nampla, lemon juice, garlic salt and chili powder mix well. Add lemon grass, red onion and chopped spring onion and coriander; toss lightly. Place mixture on serving plate, top with mint leaves, decorate with lettuce. Serve.

</td></tr>
</table>

Fried Wonton

Marx Mullinix was Lieutenant Colonel in the US Air Force when he was in Bangkok with Terry and the kids. Terry and Marx loved to eat and we even went once to the Sunday Market ground on a weekday to watch the kite fights and visited one of the oldest "Cook shops" in Bangkok. The "Fried Wonton" were one of their favorite dishes. I hope this book will find the way to them somehow.

เกี๊ยวกรอบ

ส่วน

หมูบด	1 ถ้วย
หัวหอมหั่นละเอียด	1 ช้อนโต๊ะ
ผงเกลือกระเทียม	1 ช้อนชา
น้ำปลา	½ ช้อนโต๊ะ
ผักชีหั่นละเอียด	½ ช้อนโต๊ะ
ไข่ไก่	2 ฟอง
แบ่งเกี๊ยว	1 ห่อ
น้ำมันสำหรับทอด	พริกไทยนิดหน่อย

วิธีทำ

ผสมหมูบดหัวหอมหั่นละเอียด กระ-
เทียมผงเกลือ น้ำปลาเคล้าจนเข้ากันดี
เติมพริกไทย และผักชีใส่ไข่แล้วเคล้า
ให้เข้ากันดี ห่อด้วยแบ่งเกี๊ยว จนหมด
แบ่งและไส้ ทอดในน้ำมันมากๆ จัดใส่
จานรับประทานกับซ็อสเปรี้ยวหวาน

วิธีห่อ

วางหมูบดลงบนแผ่นเกี๊ยว พับเข้าหากัน

FRIED WON TON

INGREDIENTS:

1 cup ground pork
1 tablespoon minced white onions
1 teaspoon garlic salt
½ tablespoon nampla
½ teaspoon minced coriander
1 egg
  dash pepper and MSG.
1 package Wonton skins
2 cups vegetable oil
1 egg yolk (use for seal)

METHOD:

In a bowl mix ground pork with minced white onions, garlic salt, minced coriander nampla, egg, dash with Monosodium Glutamate and pepper. Place about 1 teaspoon of pork mixture in the center of the Wonton skin. Fold over, bring the two corners around in shape of Wonton and press corners of wrapper together (seal with egg yolk).
Fry in deep hot fat for 3—5minutes. Drain on paper towel. Serve with sweet and sour sauce. (see page 16 for sweet and sour sauce)

Shrimp and ground pork toast

In July 1975 while in Honolulu, I had the occasion to cook dinner for about 60 foreign students at the East West Center, University of Hawaii on the Thai Culture Day. Of all the food prepared, this snack of shrimp and ground pork toast received the best compliment: it was gone first.

ขนมปังหน้าหมู

ส่วน

หมูบด	½ ถ้วย
กุ้งสดปอกสะอาด	½ ถ้วย
ผักชีต้นหอมหั่นละเอียด	1 ช้อนโต๊ะ
ผงเกลือกระเทียม	1 ช้อนชา
พริกไทย	½ ช้อนชา
ไข่ไก่	1 ฟอง
ผงชูรส	½ ช้อนชา
ขนมปัง	10 แผ่น
น้ำมันพืช	1 ถ้วย
ซ๊อสเผ็ด	2 ช้อนโต๊ะ

วิธีทำ

ใช้พิมพ์คุ๊กกี้รูปหัวใจกดขนมปัง จะได้
สองหัวใจต่อ 1 ชิ้นสับกุ้งให้ละเอียดดี
แล้วผสมกับหมูบด สับต่อไปจนเข้าเนื้อ
กันดีเทใส่ชาม   ผสมด้วยกระเทียมบ่น
เกลือ พริกไทย ชูรส   ผสมให้เข้ากัน
เติมผักชีต้นหอมหั่นฝอยและไข่   ใช้
ปลายซ่อมคนจนเข้ากันดีป้ายทาบนหน้า
ขนมปังจนหมด แล้วนำไปทอดในน้ำมัน
ที่ร้อนจัด โดยคว่ำหน้าลงก่อนประมาณ
2นาที แล้วกลับทอดต่อไปจนเหลืองตัก
วางไว้บนกระดาษซับน้ำมันเสริฟร้อนๆ
กับซ๊อสเผ็ด

SHRIMP AND GROUND PORK TOAST

INGREDIENTS:

½ cup ground pork
½ cup shrimp (shelled, cleaned and minced)
1 tablespoon finely chopped spring onion and coriander
1 teaspoon garlic salt
½ teaspoon pepper
1 egg
dash Monosodium Glutamate (MSG.)
1 cup vegetable oil
2 tablespoons hot sauce
10 slices bread (2 days old or stale bread)

METHOD:

In a bowl mix ground pork and minced shrimp with chopped spring onion and coriander, garlic salt, pepper, MSG. and egg.

Trim crust off bread slices and cut in desired shapes (triangles or use cookie cutter). Spread the ground pork mixture over each. Fry in deep hot fat for 2 minutes with the ground mixture side down; turn over and continue cooking for 2 more minutes until brown. Drain on paper towel. Serve hot with hot sauce.

Abalone Salad

Abalone is one of the most expensive meat in Thailand. A can of Abalone would cost almost 5 US dollars in Bangkok. It came mostly from Mexico or Southern California coast. It is probably the only dish in this cook book that is cheaper to make in the US than in Bangkok.

ยำหอยโข่งทะเล

ส่วน

หอยโข่งทะเลกระป๋อง หั่นเป็นแผ่น-
บางๆ 1 กระป๋อง

หอมใหญ่สีขาว 1 หัว หั่นเป็นวงแหวน

ผักชีต้นงามๆ 5 ต้น

ผักกาดหอมใบอ่อน 2 ต้น

กระเทียม 3 กลีบ

พริกสด 7 เม็ด

น้ำมะนาว 2 ช้อนโต๊ะ

เกลือ 1 ช้อนชา

น้ำปลา 1 ช้อนโต๊ะ

ผงชูรสนิดหน่อย

วิธีทำ

จัดผักวางเรียงใส่จาน เริ่มด้วยผักกาด
หอมและหัวหอม โรยด้วยผักชีเป็นกิ่งๆ
เรียงเนื้อหอยโข่งทะเล บนสุดเหลือ
ตรงกลางสำหรับวางน้ำจิ้ม

น้ำจิ้ม

ทุบกระเทียมและพริกให้แหลก ใส่ถ้วย
เล็กๆ เติมน้ำปลา เกลือ ชูรส และ
มะนาว คนให้เข้ากัน วางถ้วยน้ำจิ้มลง
ตรงกลางจานผักและหอยโข่งทะเล ก่อน
รับประทาน ราดน้ำจิ้มเคล้าให้เข้ากันดี
รับประทานทันที

ABALONE SALAD

INGREDIENTS:

- 1 can abalone sliced thin
- 1 large onion sliced into onion rings
- 5 sprigs coriander
- Romain lettuce (use only the young inside leaves)
- 3 cloves garlic
- 5–7 hot chili peppers
- 2 tablespoons lemon or lime juice
- 1 teaspoon salt
- 1 tablespoon nampla (fish sauce)
- Dash Monosodium Glutamate (MSG.)

METHOD:

Cut and clean Romain lettuce and arrange each leaf like a little boat on a serving plate, or small individual serving dishes. Layer with sprig of coriander, onion rings and top with sliced abalone.

In a mortar pound garlic and hot chili peppers until fine. Add nampla, salt, lemon juice and MSG, and stir until well mixed. Pour into a bowl. Place on the center of the abalone salad plate. Serve.

Spring Rolls

แป้งเปาะเปี๊ยะ

ส่วน

ไข่ 2 ฟอง   แป้งสาลี 2 ถ้วย

น้ำ ½ หรือ ¾ ถ้วย

วิธีทำ

ผสมแป้ง ไข่ และ น้ำ ตีให้เข้ากันดี
ตั้งกะทะให้ร้อนทากะทะด้วยน้ำมันนิด-
หน่อย ใส่แป้งผสมตรงกลางกะทะ และ
กรอกกะทะโดยเร็ว แป้งจะติดเป็นแผ่น
บางๆ ทิ้งไว้ในกะทะร้อนๆ ให้อยู่ตัว

EGG ROLL SKIN

INGREDIENTS:

2 eggs   2 cups flour

½ or ¾ cup water

METHOD:

Make batter with eggs, water and
flour. Beat until smooth. Grease
a 7 inch frying pan with a small
amount of oil. Heat the pan. Pour
a little batter into center bottom of
pan and quickly roll pan around so
the batter covers bottom in a thin
layer. Leave it in the hot pan just
to let it set. (about 1 minute or
less) Remove from pan and con-

46

ประมาณ 1 นาที หรือเร็วกว่านิดหน่อย
เอาแผ่นแบ้งขึ้นจากกะทะ และทำแผ่น
ใหม่โดยวิธีเดียวกันแผ่นแบ้งนี้ให้ทำให้
บางที่สุดเท่าที่จะทำได้

เปาะเปี๊ยะทอด

ส่วน
หมูบด 1 ถ้วย กุ้งต้มแล้วหั่น $\frac{1}{2}$ ถ้วย
เนื้อปู $\frac{1}{2}$ ถ้วย ถั่วงอกเด็ดหางแล้ว 1 ถ้วย
ไข่เจียวแล้วหั่นฝอย 4 ฟอง ต้นหอมหั่น
ฝอย 2 ช้อนโต๊ะ ก้านคึ่นช่ายหั่นฝอย 2
ช้อนโต๊ะ พริกไทย 1 ช้อนชา เกลือ 2
ช้อนชา เห็ดหอมหั่น 6 ดอก กระเทียม
สับ 3 กลีบ น้ำปลา 1 ช้อนโต๊ะ ซ๊อส
แม็กกี้ 1 ช้อนโต๊ะ น้ำตาล 1 ช้อนโต๊ะ
วุ้นเส้นแช่น้ำ $\frac{1}{2}$ ถ้วย แผ่นเปาะเปี๊ยะ 30
แผ่น ไข่แดง 1 ฟอง น้ำมันพืชสำหรับ
ทอด 2 ถ้วย

วิธีทำ
เจียวกระเทียมในน้ำมันเล็กน้อยผัดถั่ว-
งอกใส่หมูสับ วุ้นเส้น กุ้ง ปู ผัดให้
เข้ากันใส่ พริกไทย เกลือ ซ๊อสแม็กกี้
แล้วใส่เห็ดหอมกับไข่หั่น ผัก, ผัดให้
น้ำแห้งเทใส่จานไว้

วิธีห่อ
วางแบ้งบนเขียงตามทางขวางใส่ไส้ เป็น
ทางยาวลงบนมุมหนึ่ง พับแบ้ง ม้วนหนึ่ง
ตลบ พับริมทั้งสองข้างเข้าหากันแล้ว
ม้วนต่อไป ผนึกด้วยไข่แดง ห่อจน
หมดไส้แล้วทอดน้ำมันร้อนจัดจนเหลือง
ตักออกวางใส่กระดาษซับน้ำมัน เสริฟ
ร้อนๆจิ้มน้ำจิ้มเกี่ยวทอด หรือซ๊อสศรี
ราชาก็ได้รับประทานกับผักดิบ

tinue to make the next wrapper.
These wrappers, or thin pastry,
should be made as thin as possible.

SPRING ROLLS

INGREDIENTS:

1 cup ground pork
$\frac{1}{2}$ cup cooked shrimp chopped
$\frac{1}{2}$ cup crab meat (boiled)
1 cup bean sprouts
4 eggs slightly beaten, fried
 and chopped (see page 17)
2 tablespoons chopped green
 onion
2 tablespoons chopped celery
 leaves
2 teaspoons salt
1 teaspoon pepper
$\frac{1}{2}$ tablespoon chopped garlic
6 dried black mushrooms
 chopped (optional)
1 tablespoon nampla (fish sauce)
1 tablespoon Soy sauce
1 tablespoon sugar
$\frac{1}{2}$ cup jelly noodles (a kind of
 transparent vermicelli made
 of mung bean)
1 egg yolk
2 cups vegetable oil

METHOD:
Heat vegetable oil in frying pan.
Add chopped garlic and fry for 2
minutes. Put in ground pork, shrimp,
crab meat, bean sprouts, eggs,
green onion, celery, black mushrooms, jelly noodle. Fry for 5
minutes. Add Soy sauce. nampla,
salt and pepper.
Place about 2 tablespoons of fried
ingredients on egg roll skins. Roll
up and seal with egg yolk.
Fry in deep hot fat for 5—10 minutes, Drain on paper towel. Serve
hot.

Spicy beef with mint leaves

Larb comes from the northeastern part of Thailand, which comprise one third of the Thai population living near to the Mekhong River bordering Laos and Cambodia. The dish is very spicy and goes well with all drinks that are not sweet. Our friend Duncan Au, now a resident of Bangkok, just loves it.

ลาบเนื้อ

ส่วน

เนื้อบด	1½ ถ้วยตวง	½	กิโล
ใบสะระแหน่		10	ใบ
กระเทียม		3	กลีบ
หัวหอมแดงหั่น		1	ช้อนโต๊ะ
ลูกผักชียร่าคั่วแล้วบ่น		1	ช้อนชา
พริกบ่น		1	ช้อนชา
ข้าวคั่วบ่น		1	ช้อนโต๊ะ
ต้นหอมหั่น		1	ช้อนโต๊ะ
น้ำมะนาว		2	ช้อนโต๊ะ
เกลือ		1	ช้อนชา
น้ำปลา		1	ช้อนโต๊ะ

ผงชูรส ผักสด เช่น ถั่ว ผักกาดหอม
ผักกาดขาว ต้นเซลเลอรี่

วิธีทำ

ใช้กระดาษอลูมินั่มห่อหอมหั่นและกระ-
เทียม ย่างบนเตาไฟข้างละ 2 นาทีพอ
สุกตำให้ละเอียดพักไว้
รวนเนื้อพอสุกนิดหน่อย เทใส่ชาม
เติมเกลือน้ำปลา มะนาวผงชูรสเคล้าให้
เข้ากันใส่หอมเผากระเทียมเผา เครื่อง
เทศ ข้าวคั่วและพริกบ่นกับต้นหอมหั่น
เคล้าเบาๆด้วยซ่อมให้เข้าเนื้อกันดี เท
ใส่จานโรยด้วยใบสะระแหน่รับประทาน
กับผักสด

SPICY BEEF WITH MINT LEAVES

INGREDIENTS:

1½ cups ground beef
3 cloves garlic
1 tablespoon chopped red onion
1 teaspoon coriander seeds
    (powder)
1 teaspoon chili powder
1 tablespoon rice powder
                    (browned)
1 tablespoon chopped green
    onion
10 mint leaves
2 tablespoons lemon or lime juice
1 teaspoon salt
1 tablespoon nampla
                    (fish sauce)
    some lettuce, long green
    beans, celery stalk

METHOD:

Brown ground beef, without oil,
until the pink is gone. Place in a
mixing bowl, let cool for 5 minutes.
Using aluminum – foil, wrap the
chopped red onion and garlic. Put
it on the heat, cook until it's almost
burned. Unwrap it and pound it.
Add to the beef. Season the beef
with nampla, salt, lime juice, coriander seed, (powder) rice powder,
chili powder and green onion, Pour
the mixture into the serving plate.
Top with mint leaves. Serve with
vegetables.

Bamboo Salad

ชุปหน่อไม้

ส่วน

หน่อไม้ต้มฉีกเป็นฝอย 1 $\frac{1}{2}$ ถ้วย น้ำมะ
นาว 1 ช้อนโต๊ะ น้ำปลา 2 ช้อนโต๊ะ
ข้าวเหนียวคั่วบ่น 1 ช้อนโต๊ะ หอมแดง
เผากะเทียมเผาแล้วตำ 1 ช้อนโต๊ะ ต้น
หอมหั่นฝอย 1 ช้อนโต๊ะ ใบสะระแหน่
10 ใบ พริกบ่น 1 ช้อนชา

วิธีทำ

ใช้ปลายซ่อมฉีกหน่อไม้ให้เป็นฝอยแล้ว
ต้มให้เปื่อยประมาณ 10–15 นาที ใส่
กระชอนให้สะเด็ดน้ำพักไว้ คั่วข้าว

BAMBOO SALAD

INGREDIENTS:

$1\frac{1}{2}$ cup bamboo shoots cut into
small strips, 1 tablespoon lemon
or lime juice, 2 tablespoons nampla,
1 tablespoon sweet rice, 1 tablespoon pounded garlic and red onion,
1 tablespoon chopped green onion,
1 teaspoon chili powder, 10 mint
leaves,

METHOD:

Use the fork to shred bamboo.
Boil it for 10 to 15 minutes. Drain
and set aside. Brown the sweet
rice over medium heat until it is
golden brown, pound it and set
aside. Wrap the onions and garlic
in aluminum foil. Cook over heat

เหนียวดิบจนเหลืองแล้ว ตำให้ละเอียด
ใช้กระดาษตะกั่ว ห่อหอมแดงกับกระ –
เทียมย่างบนไฟ พอสุกแล้วตำให้แหลก
เทหน่อไม้ฉีกลงในชาม   ผสมด้วยน้ำ
ปลา มะนาว หอมกะเทียมเผาเคล้าให้
เข้ากันดี ใส่ข้าวคั่วและพริกป่น หอม
หั่นเทใส่จานโรยด้วยใบสะระแหน่ รับ
ประทานกับตับย่างและข้าวเหนียวนึ่ง

ตับย่าง

ส่วน

ตับ 1 ปอนด์ พริกไทย 1 ช้อนชา เกลือ
1 ช้อนชา ก้านผักชีหั่น 1 ช้อนชา กระ
เทียม 3 กลีบ น้ำมันพืช 1 ช้อนโต๊ะ
ไม้สำหรับเสียบ

วิธีทำ

หั่นตับเป็นชิ้น 4 เหลี่ยมขนาด 2" × 2" ตำ
ก้านผักชี กระเทียม พริกไทย เกลือ
เคล้าเข้าด้วยกันกับตับ ใส่น้ำมันพืชหมัก
ทิ้งไว้ 1 ชม. เป็นอย่างน้อย
เสียบตับไม้ละ 3 ชิ้นจนหมดย่างบนไฟ
ถ่านอ่อนๆจนเหลือง (ตับจะสุกง่าย
มาก) จัดใส่จานรับประทานกับซุปหน่อ
ไม้และข้าวเหนียว

ข้าวเหนียว

ข้าวเหนียว 2 ถ้วย   น้ำ 3 ถ้วย
ล้างทำความสะอาดข้าวเหนียวจน สะอาด
ดีแล้ว เติมน้ำให้ท่วมข้าวเหนียว นิด
หน่อยประมาณ $\frac{1}{2}$ นิ้วฟุตตั้งไฟแรง ๆ
สัก 10 นาที   ลดไฟลงให้อ่อนตั้งต่อไป
จนน้ำแห้ง.

(หรือจะหุงในหม้อข้าวไฟฟ้าก็ได้)

until almost burned. Pound.
In a mixing bowl combine bamboo,
nampla, lime juice, roasted garlic
and onion, pounded sweet rice,
chili powder, chopped green onions.
Place on a serving plate. Garnish
with mint leaves. Serve with steamed sweet rice and bar-be cue
liver.

BAR-BE CUE BEEF LIVER

INGREDIENTS:

    1 pound   beef liver
    1 teaspoon   black pepper
    1 teaspoon salt
    1 teaspoon minced   coriander
    3 cloves garlic
    1 tablespoon vegetable oil
      stick   skewers

METHOD:

Cut the liver into 2 x 2 inches
squares. Pound coriander, pepper,
salt and garlic together.   Mix with
liver. Add oil. Marinate for 1 hour.
Thread 3 pieces of liver on the
stick. Cook over charcoal until the
liver is well—done. Arrange on a
serving plate.   Serve with bamboo
salad, and steamed sticky rice.

STEAMED STICKY RICE

INGREDIENTS:

    2 cups sweet (glutinous) rice
    3 cups of water

METHOD:

Fill half a large pot with rice. Pour
in the measured amount of water.
Bring to a boil. Cover tightly and
continue cooking over very low heat
until all water has been absorbed
(about 20 minutes). Well cooked
rice will look dry and fluffy and
will feel soft when it is pressed
flat.
Serve with bamboo salad and
bar-be cue beef liver.

Cabbage Salad, Roast Chicken

Roast chicken, Northeastern style is a speciality found in a row of restaurants behind the famous Rajdumnern Boxing stadium where all Tourists go to see Thai boxing matches. It is so identified that when you refer to this dish you call it "Boxing Stadium roast chicken", just as famous as Kentucky fried chicken, I suppose.

ส้มตำกะหล่ำปลี

ส่วน

มะเขือเทศหั่น	2	ลูก
กะหล่ำปลีหั่นฝอย	1	ถ้วย
หัวแครอทหั่นฝอย	½	ถ้วย
ผิวมะนาวหั่นละเอียด	1	ช้อนชา
กุ้งแห้งบ่น	1	ช้อนโต๊ะ
น้ำมะนาว	2	ช้อนโต๊ะ
ผงกระเทียมเกลือ	1	ช้อนชา

น้ำตาล พริกบ่น ผงชูรส นิดหน่อย

วิธีทำ

ผสมผักทุกอย่างเข้าด้วยกัน ปรุงด้วย น้ำ
ตาล เกลือกระเทียม ผิวมะนาว ผงชูรส
เคล้าให้เข้ากันดี โรยด้วยกุ้งแห้ง
บ่นและพริกบ่น รับประทานกับผักสด
และ ไก่ย่าง

ไก่ย่าง

ส่วน

ไก่ 1 ตัว ตัดเป็น 4 ชิ้น

กระเทียม	3	กลีบ
รากผักชีหั่น	1	ช้อนชา

เกลือ 1 ช้อนชา พริกไทย ½ ช้อนชา

ขิงสดสับละเอียด	1	ช้อนชา
น้ำมันพืช	1	ช้อนโต๊ะ

วิธีทำ

ล้างไก่ผ่าเป็น 4 ชิ้น ผึ่งไว้
ตำรากผักชี ขิง กระเทียม พริกไทย
เกลือเข้าด้วยกัน เคล้าไก่ด้วยส่วนผสม
ทั้งหมด ใส่น้ำมันพืช 1 ช้อน หมักทิ้ง
ไว้ 1-2 ชั่วโมง อบด้วยไฟ 375° 30-40
นาที รับประทานกับส้มตำ

CABBAGE SALAD

INGREDIENTS:

  1 cup finely chopped cabbage
  2 cherry tomatoes(cut in fourths)
  ½ cup finely grated carrots
  1 teaspoon lime peel
  1 tablespoon pounded dry shrimp
  1 teaspoon garlic salt
  1 teaspoon sugar
  2 tablespoons lime juice
2-3 hot chili peppers pounded

METHOD:

Mix all chopped vegetables together.
Season with garlic salt, lime peel,
and sugar to taste. Top with pounded
chili and pounded dry shrimp. Serve
with roasted chicken.

ROASTED CHICKEN

INGREDIENTS:

  1 young chicken cut in four
    pieces
  3 cloves garlic
  1 slice ginger root
  1 teaspoon minced coriander
    root
  ½ teaspoon pepper
  1 tablespoon vegetable oil
  1 teaspoon salt

METHOD:

Pound together garlic, ginger root,
pepper, salt and coriander root. Mix
with the chicken. Add oil and marinate for 1-2 hours. Bake in 375°
oven for 30-40 minutes. Serve with
cabbage salad.

Beef Celery Salad

Marc Berent has had a colorful life; we met him in Pheonix in 1964-65 and later in Thailand when he was up country at Ubon and still later when he was US Air Force Attache to Cambodia in the 70's. Now he travels around the world for his company in California. I am quite sure that whenever he comes to Bangkok his first order after Singha Beer is this "Beef Salad", a favorite for all beer drinker.

ยำเนื้อเซลเลอรี่

ส่วน

ก้านเซลเลอรี่ฝานเป็นชิ้นบางๆ 1 ถ้วย	
เนื้อสันแล่เป็นชิ้นบางๆ	1 ถ้วย
หัวหอมแดง 1 หัวใหญ่ฝานเป็นชิ้นบางๆ	
พริกป่น	1 ช้อนชา
เกลือ	1 ช้อนชา
น้ำปลา	1 ช้อนโต๊ะ
น้ำมะนาว	2 ช้อนโต๊ะ
น้ำมันพืช	2 ช้อนโต๊ะ
ผงชูรสชนิดหน่อย	

วิธีทำ

ทอดหัวหอมครึ่งหนึ่งจนเหลือง พักไว้
รวนเนื้อในกะทะพอสุก ตักใส่ชามผสม
ด้วยก้านเซลเลอรี่ และหอมแดงสดที่
เหลือ ปรุงรสด้วยเกลือ ผงชูรส น้ำ
ปลา มะนาว เคล้าให้เข้ากันดีเทใส่จาน
เสริฟโรยด้วยพริกป่น และหอมทอด
เสริฟ.

BEEF CELERY SALAD

INGREDIENTS:

1 cup young celery – chopped
(stalk only, no leaves)
1 cup sliced beef (fillet)
1 whole red onion (sliced dia-
gonally)
1 teaspoon ground chili pepper
1 teaspoon salt
1 tablespoon nampla (fish sauce)
2 tablespoons lime juice
2 tablespoons vegetable oil
Dash Monosodium glutamate
(MSG.)

METHOD:

Brown half the onion and set aside.
Brown the beef to medium rare,
without oil. Put the beef in a bowl
and add celery, raw onion, lime
juice and fish sauce. Add a pinch
of " MSG, " to taste. Mix thoroughly.
Place on a platter, Sprinkle top
with fried onion and ground chili
pepper. Serve.

Cabbage Salad

     M.L. Terb Jumsai is probably the best known cooking authority in Thailand. She is quite widely known all over the world. Once in 1964, during one of her many trips to the U.S., she stopped by our little apartment at 1342 Sunset Drive, Tempe, Arizona, long enough to sample this dish. The verdict, I am happy to say, was very good. She also told me that the proper Thai name for this dish was "White Salad" as all the ingredients are white in color.

     For this reason, the Thai title on the opposite page is written as "White Cabbage Salad."

ยำขาว "ยำกะหล่ำปลี" หมู กุ้ง

CABBAGE SALAD WITH PORK AND SHRIMP

ส่วน

กะหล่ำปลีหั่นฝอย	2 ถ้วย
หมูต้มแล้วหั่นเป็นชิ้นเล็กๆ	½ ถ้วย
กุ้งต้ม ผ่าเป็นครึ่งซีก	7 ตัว
หอมกระเทียมทอด	1 ช้อนโต๊ะ
ถั่วลิสงคั่วบ่น	1 ช้อนโต๊ะ
น้ำมะนาว	1 ½ ช้อนโต๊ะ
น้ำปลา	1 ช้อนโต๊ะ
เกลือ	1 ช้อนชา
หัวกะทิ	¼ ถ้วย
พริกแห้งหั่นแล้วทอด	1 ช้อนโต๊ะ

วิธีทำ

ตั้งน้ำให้เดือด ลวกกะหล่ำพอสุกใส่กระชอนทิ้งไว้ให้สะเด็ดน้ำ.

ต้มกุ้งปอกผ่าเป็นสองซีก หมูเนื้อล้วนต้มหั่นเป็นชิ้นเล็ก ๆ หัวหอมแดงหั่นบางๆ ทอด กระเทียมหั่นบางๆทอดจนเหลืองพริกแห้งหั่นแล้วทอด ถั่วลิสงคั่วแล้วบ่น เทกระหล่ำปลีใส่ชามผสมด้วยเกลือน้ำปลา มะนาว เคล้าให้เข้ากันดีใส่หมูต้มถั่วลิสงราดด้วยหัวกะทิเคล้าต่อไป เทใส่ชามตบแต่งด้วยกุ้งโรยด้วยหัวหอมเจียวกระเทียมเจียว ชั้นบนสุดโรยด้วยพริกทอด

INGREDIENTS:

2 cups chopped cabbage
½ cup cooked pork finely chopped
7 medium size shrimps boiled, cut in half
1 tableapoon chopped garlic and red onion
1 tablespoon coarsely ground roasted peanuts
1½ tablespoons lemon or lime juice
1 tablespoon nampla(fish sauce)
1 tablespoon salt
½ cup coconut milk
1 tablespoon chopped dried chili (fried)
½ cup vegetable oil

METHOD:

Heat the oil in the frying pan on medium low heat. Fry the onion and garlic until brown. Set aside. Then fry the chilies.

Cook cabbage in boiling water for 2 minutes. Drain. In a mixing bowl combine cooked cabbage, salt, nam pla, lime or lemon juice, peanuts, coconut milk and cooked pork. Mix thoroughly. Place on a platter, top with cooked shrimp. Sprinkle with fried red onion, garlic and chili.

Spicy Sauce and green apple

Green mangoes are abundant in Thailand. They taste crisp and sour and are very appetising with a sweet and spicy sauce. In the states, of course, we can not find green mangoes. The best substitute I can find are green apples, the sourer the better. Most youngsters would like this dish and so would expectant mothers.

น้ำปลาหวานแอ๊ปเปิ้ล

SWEET AND SPICY SAUCE

ส่วน

แอ๊ปเปิ้ลสีเขียวสด	6	ผล
น้ำตาลทราย	1	ถ้วย
น้ำปลา	$\frac{1}{4}$	ถ้วย
กุ้งแห้งป่น	1	ช้อนโต๊ะ
พริกป่น	1	ช้อนชา
หัวหอมแดงหั่น	1	ช้อนโต๊ะ

วิธีทำ

ฝานแอ๊ปเปิ้ลเป็นชิ้นเล็กๆ แช่น้ำแข็ง
ทิ้งไว้ 10-15 นาทีเคี่ยวน้ำตาลกับน้ำปลา
บนไฟร้อนจัดๆ สัก 3-5 นาทีจนน้ำตาล
ละลายเป็นฟอง เทลงชามแก้วทิ้งไว้ให้
อุ่นจัดๆ ใส่หอมแดงกุ้งแห้งและพริกป่น
ใช้ช้อนคนให้เข้าเนื้อกัน จัดแอ๊ปเปิ้ล
ใส่จานเรียงให้สวยงามเสริฟกับน้ำปลา -
หวาน เป็นอาหารว่างหรือกับแกล้ม
เหล้าก็ได้

INGREDIENTS:

- 6 fresh green apples
- 1 cup of sugar
- $\frac{1}{4}$ cup of nampla (fish sauce)
- 1 tablespoon powdered dried shrimp
- 1 tablespoon finely chopped red onions
- 1 teaspoon chili powder

METHOD:

Cut green apples into small pieces.
Set in ice cold water for $10 - 15$
minutes. Cook the sugar and nampla over low heat for three to five
minutes, or until the sugar is melted and bubbles. Pour into a bowl;
cool for 10 minutes. Add red onion,
powdered dried shrimp, chili powder, and stir. Arrange the apples
on a flat plate. Put the sauce
in the middle of the plate. Serve as
an hors d'oevre.

Ma Hoh & Mieng Lao

The direct translation for these two accompanying dishes is "galloping horse" (Ma Hoh) and "Laotian leaf" (Mieng Lao). I do not know why it is so, but would recommend that you should find the sourest possible pineapple. The sweet pork mixture on the top will counter it.

Again these two tasty tidbits should be consumed with a "not too sweet" drink. Beer would be perfect.

ม้าฮ่อ, เมี่ยงลาว

ส่วน

หมูบด	½ ถ้วย
หัวหอมแดงหั่น	2 ช้อนโต๊ะ
กระเทียมหั่น	2 ช้อนโต๊ะ
ขิงหั่นละเอียด	1 ช้อนชา
ถั่วลิสงป่น	1 ช้อนโต๊ะ

น้ำปลา 1 ช้อนโต๊ะ กุ้งแห้งป่น 1 ช้อนโต๊ะ
น้ำตาล 1 ช้อนโต๊ะ
น้ำมันสำหรับทอด, น้ำส้มมะขาม
(น้ำมะนาว) 1 ช้อนชา ใบผักชี
พริกแดงฝานเป็นชิ้นเล็กๆ 2 เม็ด

สับปะรด	1 ผล
ขนมปัง	10 แผ่น

ใบ ผักกาดดองสำหรับห่อเมี่ยงลาว
ไม้จิ้มฟัน

วิธีทำ

รวนหมูบดในกะทะให้สุกเทใส่ชาม ทอด
หอมแดงและกระเทียม (คนละที) จน
เหลืองกรอบเทลงผสมกับหมู ผสมลง
ด้วยกุ้งแห้งป่นถั่วลิสงเคล้าให้เข้ากันใส่
น้ำปลาน้ำตาล น้ำส้มมะขาม (หรือน้ำ
มะนาว) เคล้าให้เข้ากันดี

สำหรับม้าฮ่อ หั่นสับปะรดให้เป็นชิ้น
สี่เหลี่ยมขนาด 1 ½ × 1 ½ " ตักส่วนผสม
หมูลงบนสับปะรด โรยหน้าด้วยผักชี
และพริกแดง

สำหรับเมี่ยงลาว ห่อส่วนผสมด้วยใบผัก
กาดดองจนหมดไส้และผัก ตัดขนมปัง
เป็นสี่เหลี่ยมเล็กๆ 1×1 " ทอดในน้ำมัน
จนเหลืองกรอบ วางเมี่ยงลงบนขนมปัง
ทอด เสียบด้วยไม้จิ้มฟันเป็นอาหารว่าง
หรือกับแกล้มที่ดีที่สุด

MA HOH   MIENG LAO

INGREDIENTS:

½ cup of ground pork
2 tablespoons chopped red onions
2 tablespoons chopped garlic
1 tablespoon finely chopped ginger root
2 tablespoons chopped peanuts
1 tablespoon pounded dried shrimp
1 tablespoon nampla (fish sauce)
1 tablespoon sugar
1 tablespoon lemon juice or tamarind juice
1 large pineapple
10 pieces of bread
1 cup vegetable oil
Pickled lettuce leaves
Red chilies, coriander leaves
Tooth picks

METHOD :

Cook the pork in frying pan without oil, until the pork is done. Place in a mixing bowl and set aside. Fry the red onions and garlic over low heat until crisp. Add to the pork then add dried shrimp, peanuts, ginger, sugar, nampla and lemon juice. Mix well.

FOR MA HOH :

Cut the pineapple into pieces 1½ × 1½ inches. Spoon the pork mixture on top of the pineapple. Top with coriander leaves and red pepper.

FOR MIENG LAO :

Remove crust from bread. Cut into 1 inch squares. Deep fry the bread until it is golden brown. Drain on paper towels. Wrap the pork mixture in 1 inch square pickled lettuce leaves. Put the pickled lettuce squares and bread on tooth picks.

Ham Salad

The Northern Thai has a way of preparing "tar tare" pork meat and rind sausage. It is truly uncooked by the heat, and many people are afraid to try it. Still liking the taste, but wanting to be safe, I adapt the following way of cooking this to simulate the same dish. It works quite well and many Thais are used to the idea.

แหนมเทียม

ส่วน

ไส้กรอกใส่พริก	1	ห่อ ครึ่งปอนด์
พริกบ่น	1	ช้อนชา
ขิงหั่นฝอย	1	ช้อนโต๊ะ
หัวหอมหั่น	$\frac{1}{2}$	หัว
ต้นหอมหั่น	1	ช้อนโต๊ะ
ผงเกลือกระเทียม	1	ช้อนชา
น้ำมะนาว	1	ช้อนโต๊ะ

ผักสด, ก้านเซลเลอรี่, ผักกาดหอม, ต้นหอม

วิธีทำ

หั่นไส้กรอกเป็นเส้น ๆ ใส่ชามผสมด้วย ขิงฝอย หอมหั่น โรยด้วยผงกระเทียม เกลือ น้ำมะนาว เคล้าให้เข้าเนื้อกันดี เทใส่จานโรยด้วยพริกบ่น และต้นหอม หั่นรับประทานกับผักสด

CHOPPED HAM SALAD

INGREDIENTS:

1 package chopped ham
1 tablespoon ginger-root cut into half-size matchsticks
1 teaspoon chili powder
$\frac{1}{2}$ onion sliced (half onion ring)
1 tablespoon chopped spring onion
1 teaspoon garlic salt
1 tablespoon lemon juice
Some celery stalks, lettuce and spring onions

METHOD:

Cut chopped ham into double-size matchsticks. Place in a mixing bowl. Add ginger, onion, garlic and salt.

Pour lemon juice over and mix well. Remove to a serving plate. Sprinkle top with chili-powder and chopped spring onion. Arrange raw vegetables beside and serve.

Thai Fried noodles

Another popular luncheon or late night supper dish, this Thai originated noodles dish can be found all over the country in small stalls. The caterer always moves to where the crowd congregates; at weekly markets, a theatre before and after show time, or even at some political rally. It is truly a Thai dish well known throughout the country.

ก๋วยเตี๋ยวผัดไทย

ส่วน

ก๋วยเตี๋ยวเส้นเล็ก	1	ปอนด์
(½ กิโล)		
กุ้งปอกล้างผ่าหลัง	10	ตัว
ไข่ไก่	2	ฟอง
ถั่วงอก	1	ถ้วย
ถั่วลิสงบ่น	1	ช้อนโต๊ะ
กุ้งแห้งบ่น	1	ช้อนโต๊ะ
น้ำตาล	1	ช้อนโต๊ะ
น้ำปลา	1	ช้อนโต๊ะ
ซ๊อสมะเขือเทศ	1	ช้อนโต๊ะ
กระเทียมสับ	1	ช้อนชา
น้ำมันพืช	½	ถ้วย
ต้นหอม, ผักชีหั่น	1	ช้อนโต๊ะ

พริกป่น ถั่วงอกรับประทานดิบ มะนาว
2 ชิ้น

วิธีทำ

ถ้าเป็นเส้นจันทบุรีแช่เส้นก๋วยเตี๋ยวใน
น้ำอุ่นประมาณ 10–15 นาทีแล้วผึ่งให้
สะเด็ดน้ำถั่วงอกเด็ดหางแช่น้ำ

เจียวกระเทียมให้หอม ใส่กุ้ง พอกุ้ง
สุกเติมน้ำตาล น้ำปลา ซ๊อสมะเขือเทศ
ผัดต่อไปต่อยไข่ใส่ ตีไข่แดงให้แตกเติม
เส้นก๋วยเตี๋ยว ผัดเส้นก๋วยเตี๋ยวให้เป็น
สีส้มทั่วกันใส่ถั่วงอกพอถั่วงอกสุกตักใส่
จานสำหรับเสริฟ โรยหน้าด้วยกุ้งแห้ง
ป่น และถั่วลิสงบ่น ผักชีต้นหอมหั่น
ถั่วงอกดิบใส่ข้างจานกับมะนาวตักพริก
ป่นใส่ไว้ข้างๆ รับประทานร้อนๆ 2 คน

THAI FRIED NOODLES

INGREDIENTS :

- 1 pound thai rice noodles (see glossary)
- 10 medium size shrimps shelled and cleaned
- 2 eggs
- 1 cup bean sprouts
- 1 tablespoon coarsely ground peanuts
- 1 tablespoon pounded dry shrimp
- 1 tablespoon sugar
- 1 tablespoon nampla (fish sauce)
- 1 tablespoon ketchup
- 1 teaspoon minced garlic
- ½ cup vegetable oil
- 1 tablespoon chopped spring onion and coriander leaves a sprinkle of pounded dry chili some additional bean sprouts and two pieces of lemon

METHOD:

If dry noodles are used, soak them in warm water for 15 minutes, drain. Place the bean sprouts in cold water. In a frying pan put all the oil, brown the garlic until light brown, add the shrimp and cook until well done. Add sugar, nampla, ketchup and stir together. Add eggs break in the yolk, then add noodles and fry until noodles turn orange. Lift the bean sprouts out of the water, add to the mixture and fry until bean sprouts are cooked. (about 1–2 minutes) Put on serving plate with raw bean sprouts on the side. Sprinkle top with dried shrimp, ground peanuts, and lastly chili powder. Top with green onion, coriander, and 2 pieces of lemon. Serve hot.

Mee Siam

Rex and Mary Lee Gaggino, who became our friends in Pheonix, have now moved north. Gino used to live in Singapore in his youth and remembered "Mee Siam" as one of his favorite dishes. He knew, of course, that it came from Thailand or Siam. I had great pleasure in cooking this dish for them at their house in Tempe, Arizona. Now that they have moved, we hope Mimi and Gino still have the recipe.

MEE SIAM

INGREDIENTS:

- 1 pound rice vermicelli (senmee)
- 1 cup coconut milk
- 2 tablespoons sugar
- 1 tablespoon nampla(fish sauce)
- 2 tablespoons pounded chilies
- ½ cup dried salted shrimp
- 3 tablespoons vegetable oil
- 2 tablespoons bean sauce
  some red chilies, lemon or lime, green onion, lettuce, cabbage.

หมี่สยาม (หมี่กะทิ)

ส่วน

เส้นหมี่ ½ กิโล		กุ้งแห้ง ½ ถ้วย	
กุ้งสดปอกล้างผ่าหลัง	1 ถ้วย		
หมูหั่นเป็นชิ้นเล็ก	½ ถ้วย		
ถั่วงอกเด็ดหาง	1 ถ้วย		
เต้าหู้หั่นเป็นชิ้นเล็ก	½ ถ้วย		
เต้าเจี้ยวเหลือง	2 ช้อนโต๊ะ		
หัวหอมแดงหั่น	1 ช้อนโต๊ะ		
น้ำตาล	2 ช้อนโต๊ะ		
น้ำปลา 1 ช้อนโต๊ะ		น้ำกะทิ 1 ถ้วย	
ไข่เจียวแล้วหั่น	2 ฟอง		
พริกบ่น	1 ช้อนโต๊ะ		
น้ำมันพืช	3 ช้อนโต๊ะ		

มะนาวพริกแดง ผักชี ต้นหอม ใบ
กุยฉ่าย ผักกาดหอม หัวปลี

วิธีทำ

แช่เส้นหมี่ไว้ในน้ำอุ่นประมาณ 5 นาที
ก่อนเอาขึ้นหยดสีแดงลง 3–5 หยด ผึ่ง
ไว้ในกระดาษ

ใส่น้ำมันในกะทะ ทอดหอมจนเหลือง
อ่อน ผัดถั่วงอกครึ่งหนึ่งของส่วนใส่หมี่
ผัดต่อไปอีก 5 นาที ตักใส่จานโรยหน้า
ด้วยไข่เจียวหั่น และผักชีเคี่ยวกะทิให้
แตกมันใช้น้ำกะทิสัก 3 ช้อนโต๊ะ ผัด
หมู กุ้ง จนสุกเทกะทิที่เหลือลงใน
กะทะใส่เต้าหู้หั่น กุ้งแห้ง เต้าเจี้ยว
ปรุงด้วยน้ำปลาและน้ำตาล ตักใส่ชาม
เวลารับประทานตักหน้ากะทิราดบนเส้น
หมี่ ปรุงด้วยมะนาวพริกบ่นรับประทาน
กับผักสด

---

1 cup bean sprouts
cut the following ingredients
into small pieces

½ cup pork
1 cup shelled shrimp
½ bean cake (tow hou)
1 red onion
2 eggs (fried like an omlette)

METHOD:

Soak rice vermicelli in water for 5 minutes. Before draining put in 3–5 drops of red food coloring. Heat the oil in the frying pan and fry onion until light brown; add the noodles, fry for 5 minutes; add bean sprouts and nampla.

Beat two eggs with a fork. Rub oil in clean frying pan with paper towel. Heat. pour egg into center of pan and quickly roll around so it covers bottom of pan in a thin layer. Cook over low heat until egg is done. (about 1 minute). Remove egg and cut in small strips.

GRAVY:

In soup pot, heat the coconut milk until boiling. Add shrimp, pork, dried shrimp, bean cake, bean sauce and sugar. Cook until the pork and shrimp are done.

TO SERVE:

Place the noodles on a large serving plate. Arrange the egg strips on top. Sprinkle with chopped coriander and cut red chili. Serve the gravy in separate deep bowl. Arrange a plate of raw beansprouts, with piece of lime or lemon, and other vegetables. Pound chili (or use prepared chili powder) and place in very small bowl.

Noodles in ground beef gravy

If you do not want to use the food coloring, you may substitute egg noodles for rice noodles used here. This dish is considered Thai, though the use of noodles makes it rather Chinese.

ก๋วยเตี๋ยวราดหน้าเนื้อสับ

ส่วน

สีเหลือง	5	หยด
ก๋วยเตี๋ยวเส้นใหญ่	1	ปอนด์ ($\frac{1}{2}$ กิโล)
เนื้อบด	1	ถ้วย
กระเทียมสับ	1	ช้อนชา
น้ำ	$\frac{1}{2}$	ถ้วย
หอมแดงหั่น	2	ช้อนโต๊ะ
ผงกะหรี่	1	ช้อนชา
เกลือ	1	ช้อนชา
ซีอิ๊วใส	1	ช้อนโต๊ะ
แป้งมันละลายน้ำ	2	ช้อนโต๊ะ
น้ำมัน	$\frac{1}{2}$	ถ้วย
ไข่ดาว	2	ฟอง
ผักกาดหอม	10	ใบ
ต้นหอมเซลเลอรี่หั่น	1	ช้อนโต๊ะ
พริกหั่นแช่น้ำส้ม		

วิธีทำ

ทอดไข่ดาว 2 ฟองใส่จานพักไว้
หั่นพริกสดแช่น้ำส้มพักไว้
ล้างใบผักกาดหอมสลัดให้สะเด็ดน้ำ จัด
เรียงรอบจาน ในกะทะเจียวกระเทียมพอ
หอมใส่เส้นผัดพอสุกใส่สีเหลือง3-5หยด
เทใส่จานที่เรียงไว้แล้วด้วยผักกาดหอม
ผสมน้ำกับเนื้อบดในชาม ใช้ซ่อมตีให้
เข้ากัน ในกะทะทอดหอมแดงหั่นพอสุก
เทส่วนผสมเนื้อกับน้ำผัด ต่อไปจนเดือด
ใส่ผงกะหรี่ น้ำซีอิ๊ว เกลือ ผัดต่อไป
ใส่แป้งมันละลายน้ำ ผัดต่อไปจนเดือด
ราดลงบนเส้นก๋วยเตี๋ยว ตบแต่งด้วยไข่
ดาว ต้นหอมเซลเลอรี่หั่น เสริฟร้อน
พร้อมกับพริกดอง

NOODLES IN GROUND BEEF GRAVY

INGREDIENTS:

- 5 drops of yellow food coloring
- 1 pound ($\frac{1}{2}$ kilo) rice noodles
- 1 teaspoon minced onions
- 1 cup ground beef with $\frac{1}{2}$ cup water
- 2 tablespoons chopped red onion
- 1 teaspoon curry powder
- 1 teaspoon salt
- 1 tablespoon soy sauce
- 2 tablespoons corn starch mixed with 1 tablespoon water
- $\frac{1}{2}$ cup vegetable oil
- 10 lettuce leaves
- 1 tablespoon chopped celery leaves and spring onions some pickled chili (optional)
- 2 eggs

METHOD:

Fry eggs sunny—side up; set aside. Arrange lettuce on round serving plate.

Sprinkle noodles with food coloring. In a frying pan put half of the oil, brown the garlic, add the noodles and fry well. Put noodles on the center of the arranged lettuce leaves.

FOR GRAVY

Use the remaining oil to brown the red onions; Add the meat and water mixture, and simmer for 3 minutes. Add curry powder, soy sauce, salt; stir add the corn starch and stir until gravy thickens. Spoon the gravy over noodles; top with fried eggs, then sprinkle with chopped spring onions and celery leaves, Serve hot with pickled chili.

Beef noodles soup

ก๋วยเตี๋ยวเนื้อวัว

ส่วน

เนื้อสำหรับทำสตู	1	ปอนด์ (½กิโล)
น้ำ	5	ถ้วย
พริกไทย	½	ช้อนชา
กระเทียม	3	กลีบ
อบเชยบ่น	½	ช้อนชา

BEEF NOODLES SOUP

INGREDIENTS:

- 1 pound stewing beef
- 1 pound senmee (see glossary)
- 1 quart water
- ½ tablespoon pepper
- 3 cloves garlic
- ½ teaspoon cinnamon
- 2 celery stalks

ซีอิ๊ว 1 ช้อนโต๊ะ

น้ำปลา 2 ช้อนโต๊ะ

ก้านเซลเลอรี่ (ขึ้นฉ่าย) 2 ก้าน

เนื้อสัน ตับสดหั่นบางๆ ½ ถ้วย

ลูกชิ้นเนื้อวัว 25 ลูก (ถ้าหาได้)

เส้นหมี่ 1 ปอนด์ (½ กิโล)

ถั่วงอก 1 ถ้วย

ต้นหอม ผักชี เซลเลอรี่ 2 ช้อนโต๊ะ

พริกป่นแช่น้ำส้ม (พริกป่น 1 ช้อนโต๊ะ

น้ำส้ม 2 ช้อนโต๊ะ

กระเทียมสับ 1 ช้อนโต๊ะ

น้ำมัน 2 ช้อนโต๊ะ

วิธีทำ

ในหม้อใหญ่ผสม เนื้อสตู น้ำ พริก-
ไทย กระเทียม อบเชยป่น น้ำปลา
ซีอิ๊ว ก้านเซลเลอรี่ ปิดฝาตั้งไฟจนน้ำ
เดือด ลดไฟลงให้อ่อนเคี่ยวต่อไปสัก
2-3 ชม. ตักก้านเซลเลอรี่และกลีบ
กระเทียมออก เร่งไฟให้แรงจนน้ำเดือด
รวกตับเนื้อสด ลูกชิ้นตักขึ้นใส่จานช่อง
ไว้ แช่เส้นหมี่ไว้ในน้ำอุ่นประมาณ 5
นาที ตั้งน้ำครึ่งหม้อให้เดือดรวกเส้นหมี่
และถั่วงอก จัดลงในช่องที่เหลือเวลารับ
ประทาน ตักถั่วงอกเส้นหมี่ใส่ชามตัก
น้ำซุปใส่ตามด้วย ตับ, ลูกชิ้น, เนื้อ
สด, โรยด้วยผักและกระเทียมเจียว ปรุง
รสตามชอบ.

1 tablespoon soy sauce
2 tablespoons nampla
25 meat balls (see glossary)
optional
½ cup sliced beef steak or beef
liver
1 cup bean sprouts
2 tablespoons chopped green
onion, coriander, and celery
1 tablespoon ground chili in 2
tablespoon vinegar
1 tablespoon chopped garlic
2 tablespoons vegetable oil

METHOD:

Heat the oil in a frying pan. Stir
fry chopped garlic until brown and
Put into a bowl. In a large pot,
combine beef, water, pepper, 3
cloves garlic, cinnamon, nampla,
soy sauce and celery stalks. Bring
to boil. Cover, reduce heat and simmer for 2 hours. When the meat is
tender remove garlic and celery.
Bring to the boil again, dip in sliced
beef steak and beef liver; quickly
take out and arrange on serving
plate.

Cover bean sprouts with boiling
water, drain and arrange on serving
plate. Cook Sen—mee for 2 minutes.
Drain and arrange on the serving
plate.

TO SERVE:

In individual serving bowls, put in
bean sprouts. Sen—mee, sliced beef,
liver and chopped vegetables. Pour
the broth over. Top with fried garlic
and hot chili vinegar to taste.

Indian style noodles

ก๋วยเตี๋ยวแขก

ส่วน

เนื้อสำหรับทำสตู	1	ปอนด์
		(½ กิโล)
น้ำกะทิ	2 ½	ถ้วย
หัวหอมสับละเอียด	1	ช้อนโต๊ะ
หัวหอมแดงหั่น	1	ช้อนโต๊ะ
น้ำพริกแกงกะหรี่	1	ห่อ
		(ดูหน้า 13)
ผงกะหรี่	1	ช้อนชา

INDIAN STYLE NOODLES

INGREDIENTS:

- 1 pound stewing beef
- 2½ cups of coconut milk
  (see glossary)
- 1 tablespoon minced onion
- 1 tablespoon sliced red onion
- 1 package yellow curry paste
- 1 teaspoon curry powder
- 2 tablespoons vegetable oil
- 1 teaspoon salt
- 2 tablespoons nampla
- 1 pound dry Thai rice noodles
- 1 cup bean sprouts

น้ำมัน   2 ช้อนโต๊ะ

เกลือ   1 ช้อนชา

น้ำปลา   2 ช้อนโต๊ะ

ก๋วยเตี๋ยวเส้นจันทบุรี   1 ห่อ

เต้าหู้แข็งหั่น   1 ช้อนโต๊ะ

ถั่วลิสงบ่น   1 ช้อนโต๊ะ

ต้นหอมหั่น   1 ช้อนโต๊ะ

พริกบ่นแช่น้ำส้ม (พริกบ่น 1 ช้อนชา น้ำส้ม 1 ช้อนโต๊ะ)

ไข่ต้ม (ผ่าเป็น 4 ชิ้น)   1 ฟอง

ถั่วงอก   1 ถ้วย

วิธีทำ

น้ำแกง ทอดหอมแดงจนเหลืองตักหอมขึ้นพักไว้ ใช้น้ำมันที่เหลือในกะทะผัดหอมสับกับผงกะหรี่และน้ำพริก จนหอมใส่เนื้อผัดต่อไป เติมน้ำปลา เกลือ น้ำกะทิ เทส่วนผสมใส่หม้อ ปิดฝาลดไฟให้อ่อนเคี่ยวทิ้งไว้ประมาณ 2 ชม.

แช่เส้นก๋วยเตี๋ยวในน้ำอุ่น ทิ้งไว้ประ-มาณ 15 นาที แล้วต้มในน้ำเดือดพอสุกเทลงในกระชอนพอสะเด็ดน้ำเทใส่ชามเคล้าด้วยน้ำมันพักไว้ ลวกถั่วงอกตักใส่ชามสำหรับเสริฟ (4 ใบ) ในชามเสริฟเริ่มด้วยถั่วงอกเส้นก๋วยเตี๋ยว ตักน้ำแกงใส่ โรยด้วยถั่วลิสงบ่น เต้าหู้ ผักหั่นหอมทอดและไข่ต้ม เสริฟร้อนกับพริกน้ำส้ม.

---

1 tablespoon finely diced bean cake
1 tablespoon coarsely ground peanuts
1 tablespoon chopped spring onions
1 hard boiled egg
                 (cut in fourths)
1 tablespoon chili powder mixed with 2 tablespoons vinegar.
Some vegetable oil (to sprinkle on noodles)

METHOD:

In a saucepan heat 2 tablespoons oil. Brown red onion until light brown, remove and set aside. Using the same oil, brown minced onion until light brown. Add yellow curry paste, curry powder and stir. Add the stewing beef, nampla, salt and turn until well mixed. Pour in coconut milk and bring to the boil. Lower the heat, cover, and simmer for 2 hours.

Soak the dried rice noodles in warm water for 15 minutes. Drain. Boil the rice noodles for 3 minutes, drain and sprinkle with oil to keep separate.

Cover bean sprouts with boiling water, drain and place in 4 serving dishes, Add cooked rice noodles on top of the bean sprouts. Spoon the curry mixture over each dish and garnish with diced bean cake, ground peanut, fried red onions and a piece of hard boiled egg. Top with spring onion and coriander. Serve with the chili mixed with vinegar. Makes four servings.

Noodles with sweet shrimp sauce

In the olden days, this was a favorite lunch for all Thai people. Its delicate sweet-sour flavor and mild phet make it a delight for all ages. It might interest you that the literal translation of the Thai name is "Chinese Cake and Pepper Sauce."

ขนมจีน

ส่วน

เส้นหมี่ญี่ปุ่น (Somen) 12 ออนซ์
1 ห่อ น้ำ3ถ้วย เกลือ1ช้อนชา น้ำเย็น

วิธีทำ

ต้มน้ำสามถ้วยในหม้อใหญ่ พอน้ำเดือด
ใส่เส้นหมี่ญี่ปุ่นต้มต่อไปประมาณ 3 นาที
เติมเกลือต้มต่อไปอีก 2 นาที สงเส้น
ขึ้นใส่น้ำเย็น ใช้ตะเกียบจับเส้นพันให้
เป็นวงจัดใส่จาน

น้ำพริก

ส่วน

กะทิ	2 ถ้วย
กุ้ง	1 ปอนด์
หัวหอมแดงหั่น	2 ช้อนโต๊ะ
กระเทียมหั่น	2 ช้อนโต๊ะ
ก้านผักชีหั่น	1 ช้อนชา
ใบผักชี	2-3 ช่อ
เนยถั่ว	1 ช้อนโต๊ะ
ถั่วเขียวคั่วแล้วบ่น	1 ช้อนโต๊ะ

(ถ้าไม่มีจะใช้ข้าวคั่วแทนก็ได้แต่ต้องบ่น
ให้ละเอียด)

น้ำตาล	2 ช้อนโต๊ะ
น้ำปลา	2 ช้อนโต๊ะ
น้ำมะนาว	$\frac{1}{2}$ ช้อนโต๊ะ

NOODLES WITH SWEET SHRIMP SAUCE

NOODLES

INGREDIENTS:

   1 package Japanese SOMEN
     (12 oz.)
   3 cups water
   1 teaspoon salt

METHOD:

Boil the SOMEN for 3 minutes. Add
salt, continue boiling for 2 more
minutes. Drain and rinse in cold
water to keep separate. Place on
serving plate.

SWEET SHRIMP SAUCE

INGREDIENTS:

   2 cups coconut milk
   1 pound shrimp
   2 tablespoons chopped red onion
   2 tablespoons chopped garlic
   1 teaspoon minced coriander
   2-3 sprigs coriander
   1 tablespoon peanut butter
   1 tablespoon rice powder (brown
     the rice in a dry frying pan
     and then grind or put in blen
     der)
   2 tablespoons light brown sugar
   2 tablespoons nampla(fish sauce)
   $\frac{1}{2}$ tablespoon lemon juice
   1 tablespoon chili powder
   1 cup vegetable oil

พริกบ่นละเอียด   1 ช้อนโต๊ะ
น้ำมันพืช   1 ถ้วย

วิธีทำ

ต้มกุ้งปอกผ่าหลังดึงไส้ดำออก   ตั้งกะทิ
ให้แตกมันยกลงพักไว้ให้เย็น ทอดหัว –
หอมกระเทียมให้เหลือง   แบ่งกระเทียม
ทอดไว้ต่างหากครึ่งหนึ่งคั่วถั่วเขียวหรือ
ข้าวพอเหลืองใส่ที่บด บดให้ละเอียดต่ำ
หอมทอด กระเทียมทอด   และ ก้าน
ผักชีให้ละเอียด ใส่กุ้งต้มตำจนเข้ากัน
ดีตักออกละลายน้ำกะทิ (อุ่น) เติมน้ำ –
ตาล น้ำปลา เนยถั่ว ถั่วคั่วบ่นและ
น้ำมะนาว   คนจนน้ำตาลละลายดีแล้ว
ใช้น้ำมันสัก 2 ช้อนโต๊ะ   ตั้งกะทะไฟ
อ่อนๆ ผัดพริกบ่นละเอียดพอหอม ตัก
ราดหน้าส่วนผสมกะทิตักใส่ชามโรยหน้า
ด้วยกระเทียมทอดที่แบ่งไว้   ใบผักชี
เสริฟกับขนมจีน และผักทอดกับผักสด.

ผักทอด

ส่วน

แครอท	1	หัว
ผักสลัด	$\frac{1}{4}$	หัว
ใบเซลเลอรี่	10	ช่อ
แบ่งข้าวเจ้า	$\frac{1}{2}$	ถ้วย
หัวกะทิ	$\frac{1}{2}$	ถ้วย
เกลือ	$\frac{1}{2}$	ช้อนชา

76

METHOD:

Shell and devein the shrimp. Wash
and drain.   Put coconut milk over
medium heat, bring to boil ; cook
stirring constantly for 5 minutes.
Remove from heat. Cool.

In a frying pan heat oil and brown
garlic until light brown.   Remove
garlic and set aside.   Using the
same oil. fry onion until light brown.

Remove ; place beside fried garlic.
Lower the flame and stir–fry chili
powder for 1 minute. Remove from
heat immediately. Set aside to cool.

Boil shrimp for 5 minutes.   Drain
and put into a mortar, pound toget
her with $\frac{1}{2}$ only of the fried garlic,
all of the onion and minced corian-
der.   Pound until well mixed.   Dis
solve the shrimp mixture, rice powder, peanut butter. sugar and nam
pla in warm coconut milk.   Stir well.
Adjust seasoning to taste, then
pour into a serving bowl.   Spoon
fried chili powder on top.   Garnish
coriander sprigs.   Serve cold with
noodles and vegetables.

VEGETABLES

INGREDIENTS:

1 carrot (shredded into half mat-
  chstick size)

$\frac{1}{4}$ head lettuce chopped fine

10 sprigs celery leaves

$\frac{1}{2}$ cup rice flour

น้ำมันพืช 2 ถ้วย

พริกแห้ง 5 เม็ด

วิธีทำ

ใช้ที่ฝนเนยแข็งฝนแครอทเป็นเส้นยาว
แช่น้ำเย็นไว้ ผักสลัดหั่นฝอยแช่น้ำ
เย็นไว้

ผักทอด ผสมแบ่งข้าวเจ้ากับหัวกะทิ
และเกลือละลายให้เข้ากันใส่ใบเซลเลอรี่
เป็นกิ่งๆ ชุบแบ่งให้ทั่ว ทอดในน้ำมัน
ร้อนจัดๆ (ใช้กะทะก้นลึก) พอเหลือง
ตักใส่กระดาษซับน้ำมันไว้ ลดไฟลงให้
อ่อนทอดพริกแห้งให้กรอบ จัดใส่จาน
ผักทอดจานหนึ่ง และผักสดอีกจานหนึ่ง

$\frac{1}{2}$ cup coconut milk or light cream

$\frac{1}{2}$ tablespoon salt

2 cups vegetable oil

5 dried chilies

1 pound cooked Japanese noodles (see page 6)

METHOD :

Soak carrot matchsticks and chopped lettuce in cold water. Drain and
arrange on a serving plate.
Blend rice flour in coconut milk and
salt. Mix well. Coat the celery
sprigs in batter and deep fry until
golden brown. Drain on paper
towel. Lower heat and fry chilies
until crisp. Place on a serving plate
with celery sprigs.

Noodles with fish curry sauce

น้ำยา

ส่วน

น้ำกะทิ	2	ถ้วย
น้ำพริกแกงเผ็ด (แดง)	2	ห่อ
กระชายบ่น	1	ช้อนโต๊ะ
น้ำปลาร้า (ถ้าชอบ)	2	ช้อนโต๊ะ
น้ำปลา	2	ช้อนโต๊ะ
เนื้อปลาสด	1	ปอนด์
หอมเผากระเทียมเผาตำ	1	ช้อนโต๊ะ
ขนมจีน (ดูหน้า 75)	1	จาน

NOODLES WITH FISH CURRY SAUCE

FISH CURRY SAUCE:

INGREDIENTS:

- 2 cups coconut milk (see glossary)
- 2 packages red curry paste (see page 10)
- 1 tablespoon Krachai (see glossary)
- 2 tablespoons nampla
- 1 pound halibut or cod
- Boiled SOMEN (see page 75)

วิธีทำ

ต้มปลาให้สุกตักขึ้นใส่จานพักไว้   ตั้ง
กะทิเคี่ยวให้แตกมัน (ไฟอ่อนๆ) ปอก
หอมแดง $\frac{1}{4}$ หัวหั่นเป็นชิ้นเล็ก ๆ ปอก
กระเทียม 2 กลีบห่อด้วยกระดาษตะกั่ว
ย่างบนเตาไฟ   พอสุกแก้ห่อเทใส่ครก
ตำพอละเอียด ใส่กระชายตำต่อไป เติม
น้ำพริกแกงเผ็ด ใส่เนื้อปลาต้มตำจนเข้า
เนื้อกันดี ผสมส่วนผสมปลากับน้ำพริก
ในน้ำกะทิ ใช้ช้อนค่อย ๆ คนให้ละลาย
บนๆไฟกลางพอเดือดเติมน้ำปลาน้ำปลา
ร้า (ถ้าชอบ) ยกลงรับประทานกับผัก.

ผักน้ำยา
ส่วน

ใบแมงลักงาม ๆ   10 ใบ
ถั่วงอก $\frac{1}{2}$ ถ้วย ถั่วแขกหั่น $\frac{1}{2}$ ถ้วย
ไข่ต้ม 2 ฟอง พริกบ่น 1 ช้อนโต๊ะ
ก้านผักกาดดองหั่น 2 ช้อนโต๊ะ หัวหอม
แดงหั่น 1 ช้อนโต๊ะ น้ำมันพืช 2 ช้อนโต๊ะ

วิธีทำ

ใช้น้ำมันพืชทอดหอมแดงไฟอ่อน ๆ จน
เหลืองพักไว้   ต้มถั่วงอกให้พอสุกเทใส่
กระชอนพักไว้   ต้มถั่วแขกหั่นอย่าให้
สุกมาก (เขียว) ตักใส่กระชอนพักไว้
ไข่ต้ม (5 นาที)   ปอกผ่าเป็น 4 ชิ้นต่อ 1
ฟองเรียงใส่จานช่อง ล้างใบแมงลักแช่
น้ำสลัดให้แห้งเรียงใส่อีกช่องหนึ่งจัดถั่ว
งอกต้ม   ถั่วแขกต้มโรยด้วยหอมทอด
ผักกาดดองหั่นและพริกบ่นใส่เป็นช่องๆ
เสริฟกับขนมจีนและน้ำยาร้อนๆ สำหรับ
4 คน.

1 tablespoon roasted onion and
    garlic

METHOD:

Boil the fish for 10 minutes. Drain.
Set aside. wrap the chopped onion
and garlic with aluminium foil, place
on the stove burner and cook for 2
minutes on each side.   Unwrap and
pound in a mortar with Krachai and
red curry paste until smooth.   Add
cooked fish.   Continue pounding
until well mixed. In a pot, dissolve
fish paste in coconut milk.   Cook
over medium heat to boiling point.
Add nampla. Stir until well mixed.
Remove from heat.

VEGETABLES:

INGREDIENTS:

    10 mint leaves or   "Bai mang
        luck"
    $\frac{1}{2}$ cup bean sprouts
    $\frac{1}{2}$ cup chopped   green beans
    2 hard boiled eggs cut in fourths
    2 tablespoons chili powder
    2 tablespoons   chopped red
        onions
    2 tablespoons vegetable oil

METHOD:

Heat 2 tablespoons oil and brown
the red onion until light brown. Set
aside. Boil green beans for 3 minutes. Drain and arrange on a serving dish topped with fried onion.
Boil beansprouts for 3 minutes.
Drain and put beside green beans.
Arrange hard boiled eggs, chili powder and mint leaves on the same
serving plate and serve with noodles
and fish curry sauce. Makes 4 servings.

Chow mein

Chow Mein is a Cantonese word meaning fried egg noodles. The egg noodle or "Ba-mi" has been so popular that it was accepted as Thai. You can find various combinations of egg noodles in many Chinese restaurants around the world, but the most popular among Americans is Chow Mein, which can be served as lunch or dinner.

I have retained the Chinese name due to its universality.

บะหมี่ราดหน้า (เฉาหมื่น)

ส่วน

บะหมี่สด	1	ถุง
น้ำมันสำหรับทอด	2	ถ้วย
กุ้งล้างปอกผ่าหลัง	$\frac{1}{2}$	ถ้วย
หมูหั่น	$\frac{1}{2}$	ถ้วย
เห็ดกระดุมหั่น	2	ช้อนโต๊ะ
ผักกาดเขียวหั่น (กวางตุ้ง)	1	ถ้วย
หน่อไม้หั่นเบ็น 3 เหลี่ยม	$\frac{1}{2}$	ถ้วย
น้ำปลา	$\frac{1}{2}$	ช้อนโต๊ะ
ซีอิ๊ว	$\frac{1}{2}$	ช้อนโต๊ะ
น้ำมันหอย	1	ช้อนโต๊ะ
แบ้งมันละลายน้ำ	2	ช้อนโต๊ะ

น้ำสุก $\frac{1}{2}$ ถ้วย   พริกหั่นดองน้ำส้ม

วิธีทำ

แบ่งเส้นหมี่เบ็นสองส่วน

1 ส่วนต้มในน้ำเดือดเอาขึ้นทาน้ำมันจัด
ใส่จานหนึ่งไว้ อีกส่วนหนึ่งทอดในน้ำ
มันมากๆจนกรอบ ใส่อีกจานหนึ่งไว้ใน
กะทะใช้น้ำมัน 2 ช้อนโต๊ะ ผัดกุ้ง หมู
เห็ด ผักกาดเขียว หน่อไม้ เติมน้ำสุก
ผัดต่อไปประมาณ 3 นาที เติมน้ำปลา
ซีอิ๊ว น้ำมันหอย คนจนเข้ากันดี เติม
แบ้งละลายน้ำผัดจนแบ้งสุก ตักหน้า
ราด บนเส้นหมี่ทั้งสองจาน เสริฟร้อนๆ
กับพริกดองน้ำส้ม.

PORK AND SHRIMP CHOW MEIN

INGREDIENTS:

1 package egg noodles (ba−mee)
  (see glossary)
2 cups vegetable oil
$\frac{1}{2}$ cup cut and cleaned shrimp
$\frac{1}{2}$ cup sliced pork
2 tablespoons sliced button
  mushrooms
1 cup Chinese greens cut into
  $1\frac{1}{2}''$ segments
$\frac{1}{2}$ cup sliced bamboo shoots
$\frac{1}{2}$ tablespoon nampla (fish sauce)
$\frac{1}{2}$ tablespoon soy sauce
1 tablespoon oyster sauce
1 tablespoon cornstarch (mixed
  with 1 tablespoon water)
$\frac{1}{2}$ cup hot water
2 tablespoons pickled chili
  (see page 2)

METHOD:

Boil half the noodles in hot water.
Drain, sprinkle with oil and put on
a serving plate. Set aside.
Place oil in a wok and deep fry the
rest of the noodles until golden
brown. Drain. Place on another
serving plate. Set aside. Use 2
tablespoons of the remaining oil to
stir-fry the pork, shrimp, mushrooms,
Chinese greens and bamboo shoots.
Keep turning, then add hot water
and stir−fry for 3 minutes. Add
nampla, soy sauce and oyster sauce,
turning for a few minutes. Add
cornstarch and stir until thickens.
Spoon half the mixture over the
boiled noodles, and the rest over
the fried noodles. Serve hot with
pickled chili.

Fried shrimp in batter

In Thailand, this dish would be made with fresh mussels. Twenty years ago the most famous place for this dish was a small wooden shop along Rama IV Road just beyond Lumpinee Boxing Stadium in Bangkok. It is, however, available anywhere where fresh mussels can be found.

In the U.S. I have found that shrimp is a very good substitute for mussels. An American housewife does not have to shell and clean the shrimp, for she can pick them ready for the frying pan from the frozen section in the supermarket. Do not forget to thaw before cooking.

กุ้งทอดแบ๋งหอยทอด

ส่วน

กุ้งงามๆ 10 ตัว ล้างผ่าหลังผึ่งไว้
ถั่วงอกเด็ดหาง (แช่น้ำไว้) 1 ถ้วย
ต้นหอมหั่น   1 ช้อนโต๊ะ
แบ๋งสาลี   3 ช้อนโต๊ะ
แบ๋งข้าวโพด   3 ช้อนโต๊ะ
น้ำ   ½ ถ้วย
เกลือ   1 ช้อนชา
ไข่ (ตีเบาๆ)   2 ฟอง
น้ำมันพืช   3 ช้อนโต๊ะ
ผักชี พริกไทย นิดหน่อย
น้ำพริกศรีราชาสำหรับจิ้ม

วิธีทำ

ผสมแบ๋งสาลี แบ๋งข้าวโพด เกลือ น้ำ
ตีให้เข้ากัน ใส่กุ้งต้นหอมลงไปในแบ๋ง
(ใช้กะทะเทฟลอนถ้าเป็นไปได้) ตั้ง
กะทะบนเตาเทน้ำมันลงไปจนน้ำมันร้อน
เทส่วนผสมแบ๋ง   กรอกให้ทั่วกะทะใช้
ปลายซ่อมเขี่ยกุ้งให้ได้ระยะพองาม ใส่
ไข่ทอดต่อไปให้แห้ง กลับ เพื่อทอดอีก
ด้านหนึ่งให้สุก (วิธีกลับใช้จานใบใหญ่
กว่ากะทะคว่ำลงบนกะทะ ใช้มือหนึ่งจับ
ที่ก้นจานไว้   อีกมือหนึ่งจับที่ถือกะทะ
อย่างรวดเร็วและประณีต   เทแบ๋งลงใน
จาน ตั้งกะทะบนไฟอีกทีเทแบ๋งทอดกุ้ง
ลงในกะทะทอดต่อไปอีก 3 นาที ตักใส่
จานที่เตรียมไว้ใช้น้ำมันที่เหลือในกะทะ
ผัดถั่วงอกพอสุก ตักวางบนแบ๋งทอดกุ้ง
โรยด้วยผักชีและพริกไทย รับประทาน
กับซ๊อสศรีราชา

FRIED SHRIMP IN BATTER

INGREDIENTS:

    10 large shrimp
    1 cup bean sprouts (put in
       water)
    1 tablespoon chopped green
       onion
    3 tablespoons flour
    3 tablespoons cornstarch
    ½ cup water
    1 teaspoon salt
    2 eggs slightly beaten
    3 tablespoons vegetable oil
       chopped coriander, pepper,
       and hot sauce.

METHOD:

For batter; mix flour, cornstarch,
salt and water. Shell and clean the
shrimp. Split them open from the
back. Wash well. Add shrimp
and green onion into the batter.
In frying pan heat vegetable oil
over medium heat. Pour batter
mixture all at once. Cook for 2
minutes. Add beaten egg. Cook
until just dry.
Turn over. (To do so, place a plate
larger than the frying pan over the
pan. Place one hand on the bottom
of the plate. With a quick and
neat movement, turn both over)
Replace the frying pan on the stove
and slide the shrimp in batter back
in frying pan.
Cook another 3 minutes.
Slide the fried shrimp in batter on
a pretty serving plate. In the frying
pan use the leftover oil to fry the
bean sprouts for 2 minutes. Pour
the fried bean sprouts on the top
of the fried shrimp in batter. Sprinkle with chopped **coriander** and
pepper. Serve warm with hot sauce.
This is a favorite dish among both
Thais and foreigners.

Wonton chicken soup

Wonton Soup *is probably one of the three most popular Chinese dishes in the world. I have long experimented with this soup and found this version quite agreeable to all our friends. It is a very good luncheon dish.*

เกี๊ยวไก่ตุ๋น

ส่วน

ไก่ (โคนขา)	4	ชิ้น
เห็ดหอม	8	ดอก
ขิงฝานบางๆ	2	ชิ้น
พริกไทย	7	เม็ด

WONTON CHICKEN SOUP

INGREDIENTS:

4 pieces chicken thighs
8 dried black mushrooms (see glossary)
   soaked in water for 15 minutes
2 slices ginger root

กระเทียม	2	กลีบ
รากผักชีหั่น	1	ช้อนชา
ก้านพลูบ่น	$\frac{1}{4}$	ช้อนชา
ซีอิ๊ว	2	ช้อนโต๊ะ
น้ำ	3	ถ้วย
น้ำมัน	2	ช้อนโต๊ะ
แบ๊งเกี๊ยว	20	แผ่น
หมูบด	$\frac{1}{2}$	ถ้วย
พริกไทย, ผงกระเทียมเกลือ		
ผักกาดเขียวหั่น	1	ถ้วย

วิธีทำ

ผสมหมูบดกับกระเทียมผง กับพริกไทย
ห่อด้วยแบ๊งเกี๊ยวให้หมด ต้มน้ำให้เดือด
ต้มเกี๊ยวให้สุก ตักขึ้นทาน้ำมันไม่ให้
เกี๊ยวติดกันใส่ชามพักไว้ ต้มผักกาดเขียว
พอสุกเล็กน้อยตักขึ้นใส่จานพักไว้. ตำ
พริกไทยกระเทียมรากผักชีให้ละเอียดใส่
กะทะทอดในน้ำมันพอเหลืองอ่อนๆ ใส่
ไก่ทั้งชิ้นทอดต่อไป พอไก่จวนสุกเติม
ซีอิ๊วพอน้ำเดือดเทใส่หม้อ เติมก้านพลู
บ่น ขิง เห็ดหอมบีดฝาเคี่ยวทิ้งไว้ไฟ
อ่อนๆประมาณ 1 ชม.

วิธีเสริฟ

ในชามแต่ละใบเริ่มด้วย ผักต้ม เกี๊ยว
5 ตัว, ไก่ 1 ชิ้น เห็ดหอม 2 ชิ้น น้ำ
ซุปพอท่วมตัวเกี๊ยว จะได้เกี๊ยวไก่ตุ๋น
สำหรับ 4 คน.

7 pepper corns
2 cloves garlic
1 teaspoon minced coriander
$\frac{1}{4}$ teaspoon ground cloves
2 tablespoons soy sauce
3 cups water
2 tablespoons vegetable oil
20 wonton skins
$\frac{1}{2}$ cup ground pork
$\frac{1}{4}$ teaspoon each pepper, garlic
and salt
1 cup Chinese greens cut into
2'' segments

METHOD:

In a bowl mix ground pork with
pepper, salt and garlic. Place about
teaspoon the pork mixture in the
center of the wonton skin. Fold
over, bring the two corners around
in shape of wonton and press
corners of wrapper together. Then
boil in hot water for 3 minutes,
drain, sprinkle with oil and set
aside.

In a mortar, pound together garlic.
minced coriander and pepper corn
until it becomes a smooth paste.

In a saucepan, heat 2 tablespoons
vegetable oil and brown the paste
until light brown. Add chicken.
Turn over a few times, add soy
sauce and water. Bring to a boil.
Add ground cloves, ginger and
dried black mushrooms. Cover
and simmer over low heat for 1 hour.
In a small pot boil the Chinese
greens for 3 minutes. Drain, put
into 4 serving bowls. Layer each
bowl with 5 wontons, 2 mushrooms,
1 piece of chicken and spoon the
soup over all.

Makes 4 servings.

Fried noodles
with beef and broccoli

เส้นใหญ่ผัดซีอิ๊ว,เส้นหมี่ราดหน้า

ส่วน

เส้นหมี่แช่น้ำให้นิ่ม	1	ถ้วย
ก๋วยเตี๋ยวเส้นใหญ่	1	ถ้วย
เนื้อเซอลอนสเต็กหั่นเป็นชิ้นบางๆ	1	ถ้วย
ต้นบร๊อคคอลี่งามๆ(คะน้า)	2	ต้น
เห็ดหอม	3-4	ดอก
กระเทียมสับละเอียด	1	ช้อนโต๊ะ
น้ำมันหอย	1	ช้อนโต๊ะ

FRIED NOODLES WITH BEEF AND BROCCOLI

INGREDIENTS:

1 cup Sen—mee soaked in water
(see glossary)
1 cup rice noodles
(see glossary)
1 cup Sirloin steak sliced thin
$1\frac{1}{2}$ cups sliced broccoli
3-4 dried black mushrooms
1 tablespoon minced garlic
1 tablespoon oyster sauce

ซีอิ๊วดำ 1 ช้อนโต๊ะ
น้ำปลา 1 ช้อนโต๊ะ
แป้งมันละลายน้ำ 2 ช้อนโต๊ะ
น้ำ ½ ถ้วย
น้ำมันพืช 1 ถ้วย

วิธีทำ

แช่เส้นหมี่ในน้ำอุ่นประมาณ 15 นาที
เอาขึ้นผึ่งไว้ หั่นดอกบร๊อคคอลี่เอาดอก
ไว้ทางส่วนก้านปอกเปลือกแล้วฝานเป็น
ชิ้นบางๆแช่น้ำไว้ เนื้อใช้เซอลอนสเต็ก
หั่นเป็นชิ้นบางๆ แบ่งเป็น 2 ส่วน เห็ด
หอมแช่น้ำพอนิ่มเอาขึ้นไว้กับดอกบร๊อค
คอลี่

ผัดซีอิ๊ว ใช้น้ำมันครึ่งถ้วยเจียวกระ-
เทียมครึ่งหนึ่งให้หอม ใส่เนื้อส่วนหนึ่ง
ผัดต่อไป 2 นาที ใส่ก้านบร๊อคคอลี่ผัด
ต่อไป พอผักสุกเติมเส้นผัดต่อไปจน
เข้าเนื้อกันดี เติมน้ำปลา ซีอิ๊ว พอเส้น
เหลืองทั่วแล้ว ตักใส่จานใช้ปลายซ่อม
เขี่ยผักและเนื้อให้อยู่ข้างบน เสริฟ
ร้อนๆ

ผัดราดหน้า ใช้น้ำมัน 2 ช้อนโต๊ะเจียว
กระเทียมที่เหลือพอเหลือง ใส่เส้นหมี่
ผัดต่อไปสัก 3 นาที ตักใส่จานไว้
ในกะทะใช้น้ำมันที่เหลือ ผัดเนื้อ ดอก
บร๊อคคอลี่ และเห็ดเติมน้ำพอเดือดใส่
น้ำมันหอย น้ำปลา เติมแป้งพอแบ่งสุก
ตักราดหน้าเส้นหมี่ เสริฟร้อนๆ กับ
พริกดองน้ำส้ม.

1 tablespoon Chinese soy sauce
1 tablespoon nampla
1 tablespoon cornstarch mixed
   with 1 tablespoon water
½ cup water
1 cup vegetable oil.

METHOD:

Soak Sen—mee in warm water for 15
minutes. Drain. Set aside. Break
the broccoli into individual branches
or sprigs and slice the broccoli
stalks into thin pieces. Soak in cold
water for 15 minutes. Slice the
beef into thin pieces.

PAT SEE—IW: Place in a frying
pan ½ cup oil. Brown ½ tablespoon garlic until light brown. Add
half of the sliced beef and stir—fry
for 2 minutes. Add half the amount
of broccoli. Turn over a few times.
Add the rice noodles, soy sauce
and ½ tablespoon nampla. Stir—fry
until noodles are brown. Place on
a serving plate. Serve hot.

PAT RATNA: In frying pan use 2
tablespoons oil to cook minced
garlic to light brown. Add Sen—mee.
Stir—fry for 3 minutes. Place on
serving plate. Heat the remaining
oil. add beef. broccoli and black
mushrooms. Stir—fry for 3 minutes. Add water and bring to boil.
Add oyster sauce and nampla; add
cornstarch and stir until thickens.
Spoon over Sen—mee. Serve with
pickled chili. (see page 2)

Bamee and Senyai num

บะหมี่แห้ง

ส่วน

บะหมี่สำเร็จรูป 2 ซองหรือบะหมี่สด 4 ก้อน น้ำมัน 2 ช้อนโต๊ะ ถั่วงอก $\frac{1}{2}$ ถ้วย กระเทียมสับ 1 ช้อนโต๊ะ หมูแดงหั่น (ดูวิธีทำหน้า 147) 10 ชิ้น น้ำปลา 1 ช้อนโต๊ะ ตั้งฉ่าย $\frac{1}{2}$ ช้อนโต๊ะ ต้นหอมผักชีหั่น $\frac{1}{2}$ ช้อนโต๊ะ

วิธีทำ

กระเทียมเจียวจนเหลือง ตักใส่ชามพัก เอาไว้ต้มเส้นบะหมี่จนสุก ใช้ตะเกียบ คีบใส่ชามเคล้าด้วยน้ำมันในกระเทียม

YELLOW NOODLE WITH ROASTED PORK

INGREDIENTS:

- 2 packages egg noodles or $\frac{1}{2}$ pound fresh egg noodles (see glossary)
- $\frac{1}{2}$ cup bean sprout
- 2 tablespoons vegetable oil
- 1 tablespoon minced garlic
- 10 slices roast pork (see page)
- $\frac{1}{2}$ tablespoon dried salty lettuce
- 1 tablespoon nampla (fish sauce)
- 1 tablespoon chopped spring onions and/or coriander

เจียวให้เข้ากันดีกินน้ำปลา ตั้งฉาย เท
ใส่จานสำหรับเสริฟ ต้มถั่วงอกพอสุก
ตักใส่กระชอนพอสะเด็ดน้ำ ต้องจัดวาง
ไว้ข้างๆบะหมี่ วางหมูแดงบนเส้นบะหมี่
โดยรอบ โรยหน้าด้วยต้นหอมผักชีหั่น
และกระเทียมเจียว สำหรับ 2 คน.

ก๋วยเตี๋ยวเส้นใหญ่น้ำ

ส่วน

ก๋วยเตี๋ยว เส้นใหญ่	½	กิโล
ถั่วงอก	1	ถ้วย
น้ำต้มไก่	2½	ถ้วย
หมูต้มหั่นเบนชิ้นๆ	12	ชิ้น
ลูกชิ้นปลา	6	ลูก
หมูบด	2	ช้อนโต๊ะ
ตั้งฉาย	1	ช้อนชา
กระเทียมสับ	½	ช้อนโต๊ะ

ต้นหอมผักชีหั่น 1 ช้อนโต๊ะ น้ำมันพืช
พริกป่น, น้ำตาล, ถั่วลิสงป่น, น้ำปลา
อย่างละ 1 ช้อนโต๊ะ
น้ำส้มพริกดอง (ดูหน้า ......)
วิธีทำ
ลวกถั่วงอกพอสุกตักใส่ชามใหญ่สำหรับ
เสริฟ ลวกเส้นก๋วยเตี๋ยวพอสุกตักใส่ชาม
ที่รองด้วยถั่วงอกตั้งน้ำมันเจียวกระเทียม
พอเหลือง ราดลงบนเส้นก๋วยเตี๋ยวตั้ง
น้ำกระดูกไก่จนเดือด ใช้ช้อนตักหมูบด
หยอดลงเป็นก้อนเล็กๆ จนหมดใส่ลูก –
ชิ้นปลา เติมน้ำปลา ตั้งฉาย เทราด
ลงในชามที่ใส่เส้นก๋วยเตี๋ยว ตบแต่ง
ด้วยหมูต้มและผักชีต้นหอม เสริฟกับน้ำ
ส้ม พริกดอง และ พริกป่นน้ำตาล
ถั่วลิสงป่นสำหรับปรุงรสสำหรับ 2 คน.

METHOD :

Heat 2 tablespoons oil. Brown the
garlic until light brown. Pour into
a small bowl and set aside.
Boil the noodles for 10 minutes.
Drain and rinse in cold water Boil
the bean sprouts for 5 minutes.
Drain and place on 2 serving dishes.
Layer with noodles, fried garlic, sliced
pork, dried salty lettuce and top
with chopped spring onions and cori
ander. Makes 2 servings.

RICE NOODLES WITH PORK SOUP

INGREDIENTS:

    1 pound rice noodles, big strips
    1 cup bean sprouts
    2½ cups chicken broth
    12 slices cooked pork
    6 fish balls (optional)
    2 tablespoons ground pork
    1 tablespoon nampla (fish sauce)
    1 teaspoon dried salty lettuce
    ½ tablespoon minced garlic
    1 tablespoon vegetable oil
    1 tablespoon chopped spring
    onions and/or coriander
    1 tablespoon each—chili powder,
    sugar and ground peanuts
    pickled chili (see page 6)

METHOD :

Boil the bean sprouts for 5 minutes.
Drain and place in serving bowl.
Boil the noodles for 5 minutes.
Drain and place on top of the cooked
bean sprouts. Brown the garlic in 1
tablespoon vegetable oil until light
brown. Pour over noodles. Heat
the chicken broth in a sauce pan.
Drop in the ground pork. Add fish
balls, nampla and dried salty lettuce.
Pour over the noodles. Garnish with
sliced pork and the green vegetable.
Serve with chili powder, sugar, ground
peanut and pickled chili. Makes 2
servings.

Dumpling

บนมจีบ

ส่วน

แบ่งห่อเกี๊ยว 1 ห่อ   หมูบด 1 ถ้วย
หน่อไม้หั่นละเอียด, ซีอิ๊วใส อย่างละ
2 ช้อนโต๊ะ หัวหอมสับละเอียด, กุ้ง
แห้งป่น, น้ำปลา อย่างละ 1 ช้อนโต๊ะ
ผักชีหั่นละเอียด 1 ช้อนชา พริกไทย$\frac{1}{4}$
ช้อนชา ไข่ไก่ 1 ฟอง ผงชูรส

วิธีทำ

ผสม หมูบด, หน่อไม้, หอมสับ, กุ้ง

DUMPLING

INGREDIENTS :

1 package Wanton skin
1 cup ground pork
2 tablespoons bamboo shoots
   dice into small pieces
1 tablespoon minced onions
$\frac{1}{2}$ teaspoon garlic powder
1 tablespoon nampla
1 teaspoon coriander
1 tablespoon pounded dried
   shrimp   1 egg
2 hard boiled eggs yolk from
   cut fine
2 tablespoons soy sauce
Dash of pepper and (MSG)

METHOD :
In a mixing bowl, combine ground
pork, bamboo shoots, onions, dried

แห้งป่น, ผงกระเทียม น้ำปลา, ผักชี
หั่น พริกไทย, ผงชูรสเข้าด้วยกันต่อย
ไข่ใส่ คนต่อไปจนเข้าเนื้อกันดี ใช้ช้อน
ตักไส้ประมาณ 1 ช้อนโต๊ะวางบนแบ่ง
เกี๋ยวห่อให้เป็นรูปถ้วยเล็กๆ ใช้กรรไกร
ขลิบปลาย แบ่งทิ้งโรยหน้าด้วยไข่แดง
เรียงใส่รังถึง รองรังด้วยใบตองหรือ
กระดาษตะกั่วทาน้ำมัน นึ่งประมาณ 10
นาที เสริฟร้อนๆ จุ่มกับซีอิ๊วใส.

ก๋วยเตี๋ยวหลอด

ส่วน

ก๋วยเตี๋ยวเส้นใหญ่ (เป็นแผ่นๆ) ½ กิโล
หมูบด 1 ถ้วย เห็ดสดหั่นบางๆ ½ ถ้วย
ถั่วงอก ½ กิโล ผงกระเทียมเกลือ, ผัก
ชีหั่นละเอียด อย่างละ 1 ช้อนชา เห็ด
หอมแช่น้ำหั่นเป็นชิ้นเล็ก ๆ, หัวหอม
สับละเอียด, ซีอิ๊วใส, กุ้งแห้งป่น,
กระเทียมอย่างละ 1 ช้อนโต๊ะ พริกไทย
½ ช้อนชา ไข่ไก่ 1 ฟอง น้ำมันพืช
2 ช้อนโต๊ะ

วิธีทำ

ใช้ไฟอ่อนตั้งน้ำมัน เจียวกระเทียมพอ
เหลืองอ่อนๆ พักไว้ลวกถั่วงอกให้พอสุก
ตักใส่กระชอนทิ้งไว้จนสะเด็ดน้ำ เท
ใส่ชามผสมลงด้วยหมูบด เห็ดสดเห็ด
หอม หอมสับกระเทียมผงเกลือ ผักชีหั่น
ละเอียด พริกไทย ซีอิ๊ว ผสมทุกอย่าง
ให้เข้ากันดี ต่อยไข่ใส่คนต่อไปแล้วตัก
ไส้ใส่แผ่นก๋วยเตี๋ยว ห่อให้เป็นหลอด
ยาวๆคล้าย ๆ ไส้กรอกเส้นผ่าศูนย์กลาง
1'' จนหมดไส้ เรียงใส่รังถึงโรยด้วยกุ้ง
แห้งป่นเป็นทางยาว นึ่งประมาณ 15-20
นาที เรียงใส่จานใช้กรรไกรตัดเป็นคำๆ
โรยหน้าด้วยกระเทียมเจียว เสริฟร้อนๆ
จุ่มกับซีอิ๊วใส.

shrimp, garlic powder, nampla,
coriander, pepper, MSG and one
egg. Mix well. Place about 1
teaspoon of the ground pork mixture in the center of each wanton
skin. Shape into a small cup. Trim
the edges with kitchen scissors and
top with egg yolk. Steam for 10
minutes. Serve hot with soy sauce.
Make 2 dozen.

GROUND PORK NOODLE ROLLS

INGREDIENTS:

    1 pound uncut, sliced noodle
        or egg roll skin (see glossary)
    1 cup ground pork
    ½ cup beansprouts
    ½ cup sliced mushrooms
    1 tablespoon sliced thin, dried
        black mushrooms
    1 tablespoon minced onion
    1 teaspoon garlic salt
    1 tablespoon soy sauce
    ½ teaspoon pepper
    1 tablespoon pounded dried
        shrimp   1 egg
    1 teaspoon minced coriander
    2 tablespoons fried chopped garlic

METHOD:

Boil the beansprouts for 3 minutes.
Drain.

In a mixing bowl combine pork,
cooked beansprouts, 2 kinds of
mushrooms, minced onion, garlic,
salt, pepper, soy sauce and egg.
Mix well.

Place about 3 tablespoons of the
pork mixture on uncut noodles (or
egg rol skin). Roll up and seal
with beaten egg. Place into a
Steamer. Sprinkle top with pounded
dried shrimp. Steam for 15—20
minutes. Place on a serving plate.
Cut with kitchen scissor. Garnish
with fried garlic.
Serve hot with soy sauce

Steamed Buns

      This is another Chinese specialty that we Thais like so much, which, like the dumpling, we adapt to our kitchen. Here we use "biscuit" dough to make the bun, instead of preparing the flour in the Chinese way.

ชาละเป่า

ส่วน

หมูบด	1	ถ้วย
หัวหอมสับละเอียด	2	ช้อนโต๊ะ
เห็ดหอมหั่นละเอียด	1	ช้อนโต๊ะ
หน่อไม้หั่นละเอียด	1	ช้อนโต๊ะ
ผงกระเทียมเกลือ	1	ช้อนชา
พริกไทย	$\frac{1}{4}$	ช้อนชา
ผักชีหั่นฝอย	1	ช้อนชา
ซ๊อสแม๊กกี้	1	ช้อนชา
ไข่ไก่ต้ม	2	ฟอง
แบ่ง	2	กระป๋อง

Pillsbury Buttermilk Biscuits
กระดาษขาวตัดเป็นชิ้นเล็ก 2×2" 20 แผ่น
น้ำมันพืช 2 ช้อนโต๊ะ ผงชูรส

วิธีทำ

ในกะทะใส่น้ำมันพืช 1 ช้อนโต๊ะ ผัด
หัวหอมสับให้หอมแล้วใส่หมูบด เห็ด
หอมหั่น ผัดจนหมูสุกใส่ผงกระเทียม
เกลือพริกไทย ผักชีหั่น ชูรส ซ๊อส
แม๊กกี้ ผัดต่อไปจนเข้าเนื้อกันดีตักใส่
จานพักไว้ 10 นาที พอเย็นห่อด้วยแบ่ง
Biscuits ตัดไข่ต้มเป็นชิ้นเล็กๆ (1ลูก
8 ชิ้น) วางตรงกลางไส้ ห่อเป็นลูก
กลมๆ วางบนกระดาษแผ่นเล็กๆทาด้วย
น้ำมันจัดวางในรังถึงนึ่งประมาณ10นาที
จะได้ชาละเป่า 20 ลูก.

STEAMED BUNS WITH PORK FILLING (Salapaw)

INGREDIENTS:

    1 cup ground pork
    2 tablespoons chopped onion
    1 tablespoon chopped dried
        black mushrooms
    1 tablespoon diced bamboo
        shoots
    1 teaspoon garlic salt
    1 teaspoon minced coriander
    1 teaspoon Maggie sauce
        dash of monosodium glu-
        tamate (MSG)
    2 hard boiled eggs cut into 10
        pieces each
    2 tablespoon vegetable oil
   20 papers cut 2x2''
    2 cans Pillsbury Buttermilk
        Biscuits

METHOD:
In a frying pan heat 1 tablespoon
oil. Stir—fry onion, ground pork
and dried black mushrooms for 5
mins. Add garlic, salt,.sprinkle with
MSG. pepper, Maggie sauce and
coriander, tossing lightly until well
mixed. Spoon into a bowl. Cool.
Shape biscuit dough into small
cups and fill with pork mixture
topped with a piece of hard boiled
egg. Wrap into small balls and put
on pieces of paper rubbed with oil.
Arrange in a steamer. Steam for
10 mins. Makes 20 Salapaw.

Panang meat balls

There are three dishes in this picture, Panang Meatballs in the center, Chicken In Coconut Soup in front, and Stuffed Crab Meat in the plate near the top left.

"Panang" denotes a thicker kind of kang phet (red curry) with ground peanut added, but all vegetables left out. It can be made with beef or chicken. However, if you use chicken, do not cut into small pieces, or it will fall apart.

If you drain away the sauce after cooking, the meatballs can be served as a delicious and spicy cocktail food.

พแนงลูกชิ้นเนื้อ

ส่วน

เนื้อบด	½	กิโล
แป้งสาลี	½	ถ้วย
น้ำพริกแกงแดง	2	ช้อนโต๊ะ
ถั่วลิสงบ่นหรือเนยถั่ว	2	ช้อนโต๊ะ
น้ำปลา	1	ช้อนโต๊ะ
น้ำตาล	1	ช้อนโต๊ะ
ใบโหระพา		
น้ำมันพืช	2	ช้อนโต๊ะ

วิธีทำ

ปั้นเนื้อบดให้เป็นก้อนกลม เส้นผ่าศูนย์
กลาง 1 นิ้ว เคล้าลงในแป้งสาลี ทอด
ในน้ำมันไฟอ่อน ๆ พอให้ผิวลูกชิ้นสุก
ตักลูกชิ้นออกจากกะทะ ใช้น้ำมันที่
เหลือผัดน้ำพริกให้หอมใส่กะทิซึ่งเคี่ยว
จนแตกมันแล้ว ปรุงด้วย น้ำปลา น้ำ
ตาล เนยถั่ว ใส่ลูกชิ้นลงไปเคี่ยวจน
ลูกชิ้นสุกตักใส่ชามโรยด้วยใบโหระพา.

PANANG MEAT BALLS

INGREDIENTS:

1 pound (½ kilo) ground beef
¼ cup flour
1 cup coconut milk
2 tablespoons red curry paste
 (see page 12)
1 tablespoon nampla
 (fish sauce)
2 tablespoons peanut butter
1 tablespoon sugar
2 tablespoons vegetable oil
10 sweet basil leaves or mint
 leaves (optional)

METHOD:

Shape the ground beef into 1 inch
round balls and roll the meat balls
in flour. Fry until brown, keep
rocking the pan constantly to keep
evenly round. Use the leftover oil
in the frying pan to fry the curry
over low heat for 2 minutes. Add
cooked coconut milk. Stir together.
Add peanut butter, sugar, nampla
and meat balls, cook until the
meat Is done. Place in serving
dish. Sprinkle top with sweet basil
or mint leaves.

Among the most popular Thai dishes is this Chicken in Coconut Soup. What is so distinctive about the taste is the presence of "Kha" in the ingredients. If you are in the Los Angeles area, "Chuladul Thai Restaurant" in Culver City serves a very creditable "Chicken in Coconut Soup".

ไก่ต้มข่า

ส่วน

เนื้ออกไก่ล้วน ๆ	1	ถ้วย
ข่าอ่อนหั่นเป็นแว่น ๆ	1	ช้อนโต๊ะ
น้ากะทิ	2	ถ้วย
น้ำมะนาว	2	ช้อนโต๊ะ
น้ำปลา	2	ช้อนโต๊ะ
พริกป่น	1	ช้อนชา
ผักชี นิดหน่อย		

วิธีทำ

เคี่ยวไก่ในน้ำกะทิจนแตกมัน ใส่ข่าพอ สุกเทใส่ชาม ปรุงด้วยมะนาว น้ำปลา โรยหน้าด้วยพริกป่นและผักชี รับประ- ทานร้อนๆ

CHICKEN IN COCONUT SOUP

INGREDIENTS:

- 1 cup sliced chicken breast
- 2 cups coconut milk
- 2 tablespoons nampla(fish sauce)
- 2 tablespoons lemon or lime juice
- 1 tablespoon of sliced kha (see glossary)
- 1 tablespoon pounded chili and coriander leaves

METHOD :

Cook chicken in coconut milk. Add sliced kha. Cook until chicken is tender. Pour in serving dish. Sea- -son with nampla and lemon juice. Sprinkle top with chili powder and coriander leaves. Serve hot.

The English translation of "Pu Cha" is literally "Dearest Crab". We like to think that this dish is so endearing that it deserves such a tender name. It is of course very tasty and so easy to make that you will certainly not forget the name "Pu Cha"

ปูจ๋า

ส่วน

หมูบด	½	ถ้วย
เนื้อปู (นึ่ง)	½	ถ้วย
ไข่	1	ฟอง
หัวหอมหั่นละเอียด	1	ช้อนโต๊ะ
ขนมปัง	1	แผ่น
นมสดกระป๋อง	¼	ถ้วย
ผงกระเทียมเกลือ	1	ช้อนชา
พริกไทย	นิดหน่อย	
ผักชีหั่นละเอียด	½	ช้อนโต๊ะ
ใบผักชี พริกแดง	สำหรับแต่งหน้า	
น้ำมันพืช	2	ถ้วย
ผงชูรส	½	ช้อนชา

วิธีทำ

ฉีกขนมปังเป็นชิ้นเล็กๆ แช่ลงในน้ำนม ผสมเข้าด้วยกัน หมูบด เนื้อปู กระ-เทียมเกลือผงชูรส คนให้เข้ากันดี ใส่ไข่และขนมปังแช่นม เติมผักชีหั่น หัว หอมพริกไทย เคล้าจนเข้าเนื้อกันดีแล้ว ตักใส่เปลือกหอย, กระดองปู หรือปั้น เป็นก้อน ตบแต่งหน้าด้วยใบผักชีพริก แดง นึ่งประมาณ 25 นาที ทิ้งไว้จนเย็น ทอดในน้ำมันมากๆ จนเหลือง จัดใส่ จาน

STUFF CRAB MEAT

INGREDIENTS :

½ cup ground pork
½ cup crab meat (boiled)
1 egg
1 tablespoon chopped white onion
1 piece of bread
¼ cup milk
1 teaspoon garlic salt
½ teaspoon pepper
½ tablespoon chopped coriander leaves and red chili
2 cups vegetable oil

METHOD :

Soak bread in milk. Mix crab meat with ground pork, garlic salt, egg, bread and milk mixture. Add chopped coriander and chopped onion. Mix well. Put mixture in the crab shells or clam shells. Top with coriander leaves and sliced red chili. Steam them for 30 minutes. Let Pu cha cool. Fry in hot oil until brown.

Beef curry

BEEF CURRY WITH PUMPKIN

แกงเผ็ดเนื้อใส่ฟักทอง

ส่วน

เนื้อหั่นเบนชั้น	1 ถ้วย		
ฟักทองปอกเปลือกหั่นเบ๋น	4 เหลี่ยม		
เล็กๆ 1 ถ้วย	กะทิ 2 ถ้วย		
เครื่องแกงเผ็ด 2 ห่อหรือ	2 ช้อนโต๊ะ		
พริกสดหั่น	2 เม็ด		
ใบโหรพาหรือใบพริก	10 ใบ		
น้ำปลา	2 ช้อนโต๊ะ		
น้ำมันพืช 2 ช้อนโต๊ะ	ผงชูรส		

INGREDIENTS :
1 cup beef sliced thin
2 cups coconut milk or light cream
1 cup pumpkin peeled and diced
2 packages or 2 tablespoons red curry paste (see page 12)
2 chilies cut lengthwise
10 sweet basil leaves or chili leaves
2 tablespoons nampla (fish sauce)
2 tablespoons vegetable oil

METHOD :
In a sauce pan heat oil over low heat. Stir—fry red curry paste for 3 minutes. Add sliced beef and nampla. Turn over a few times.

วิธีทำ

กะทะตั้งไฟอ่อน ๆ ใช้น้ำมันพืชผัดพริก
แกงจนหอมใส่เนื้อ น้ำปลา ผงชูรสผัด
จนเนื้อสุกใส่กะทิ เทใส่หม้อปิดฝาตั้ง
ไฟอ่อน ๆ เคี่ยวทิ้งไว้ประมาณ 20 นาที
ใส่ฟักทองเคี่ยวต่อไป จนฟักทองสุกใส่
พริกสดหั่นและใบโหรพา หรือใบพริก
ยกลง.

หมูกรอบ

ส่วน

เส้นหมี่ 1 แพ (8ออนซ์)
หมูหั่นๆชิ้นเล็กๆ 2 ช้อนโต๊ะ
น้ำปลา 2 ช้อนโต๊ะ เต้าเจี้ยว 1 ช้อนโต๊ะ
น้ำตาล 2 ช้อนโต๊ะ น้ำมันพืช 2 ถ้วย
ไข่ 1 ฟอง กุ้งสดปอกผ่าหลังหั่น ½ ถ้วย
ต้นหอมหั่น 1 ช้อนโต๊ะ
ถั่วงอก ½ ถ้วย ผงกระเทียม 1 ช้อนชา
ผิวส้มซ่าหั่น (ผิวมะนาว) 1 ช้อนชา
ใบผักชี และพริกแดงหั่นตามยาว 1 เม็ด

วิธีทำ

ใช้น้ำร้อนลวกเส้นหมี่แล้วเทน้ำออกผึ่ง
ไว้ให้แห้ง ใช้น้ำมันมากๆ กะทะก้นลึก
ทอดเส้นหมี่ไฟอย่าร้อนจัด พอเส้นพอง
เหลืองกลับอีกข้างหนึ่งพอเหลือง ช้อน
เอาขึ้นพักไว้ ใช้น้ำมันครึ่งถ้วยผัดกุ้ง
หมูโรยด้วยผงกระเทียมพอหมูสุกเติม น้ำ
ตาล น้ำปลา เต้าเจี้ยวผัดให้เดือดต่อย
ไข่ใส่ใช้ปลายตะหลิวตีไข่แดงให้แตกคน
ให้เร็ว ๆ ให้ไข่แยกจากกันบิเส้นหมี่ใส่
ให้หมดใช้พายคนเบาๆ ให้เข้าเนื้อกันดี
เทใส่จานวางถั่วงอกไว้ข้างๆ โรยด้วยผิว
ส้มซ่า (หรือผิวมะนาว) ใบผักชีและ
พริกแดงหั่น.

Add coconut milk and stir until well
mixed. Cover and let simmer for
20 minutes. Add pumpkin, cooking
over medium heat until pumpkin is
tender. Add chilies and sweet basil leaves. Remove from heat.

CRISPY NOODLES

INGREDIENTS:

   1 package 8 ounce Sen–mee
   2 cups vegetable oil
   ½ cup shrimp shelled, cleaned
      and cut into small pieces
   2 tablespoons sliced lean pork

   1 tablespoon brown bean sauce
   2 tablespoons nampla (fish
      sauce)
   2 tablespoons sugar
   1 egg
   1 tablespoon chopped spring
      onion
   ½ cup beansprouts
   1 teaspoon grated lemon rind
   1 teaspoon garlic–powder
   3 sprigs coriander and red chili
      cut lengthwise

METHOD:

Scald Sen–mee in boiling water.
Drain and leave in strainer to dry
out for 5 minutes. Fry Sen–mee
in deep-fat until light brown. Remove
and set aside.

In a wok heat 3 tablespoons of
remaining oil over medium heat.
Fry shrimp and pork, sprinkle with
garlic–powder and continue to stir-
fry for a few minutes. Add sugar,
brown bean–sauce and nampla.
Turn over a few times. Add egg
and stir-fry until the egg is almost
cooked. Add fried Sen–mee tossing
lightly until well mixed. Sprinkle top
with grated lemon rind. Put beansprouts beside Mee grob. Garnish
with coriander sprigs and red chili.

Chicken curry

Peter K. Abbey and his family were in Bangkok for less than a year in 1969, Peter was a member of General Research Corporation Team. He and wife Lynn learned to like Thai food tremendously. In our two visits to the West Coast, we managed to do some Thai cooking for them. This chicken curry is certainly Peter's favorite Thai dish. By now, Lynn is probably the best cook of Thai food in Santa Barbara, California.

แกงเขียวหวานไก่

ส่วน

เนื้อไก่ล้วนหั่น	1 ถ้วย
เครื่องแกงเขียวหวาน	2 ห่อ
หรือ 2 ช้อนโต๊ะ (ดูวิธีทำหน้า 13)	
เม็ดถั่วลันเตาเม็ดเล็ก	1 ถ้วย
พริกสด (หั่น)	2 เม็ด
น้ำปลา 2 ช้อนโต๊ะ	กะทิ 2 ถ้วย
น้ำมันพืช 2 ช้อนโต๊ะ	ผงชูรส

วิธีทำ

ใช้น้ำมันผัดพริกแกงให้หอม ใส่ไก่โรย
ผงชูรสและน้ำปลา ผัดต่อไปจนไก่สุก
เติมน้ำกะทิพอเดือดใส่เม็ดถั่วลันเตาและ
พริกสดพอเดือดยกลง.

ยำไข่เค็ม

ส่วน

ไข่เค็ม (ดูวิธีทำหน้า 19)	3 ฟอง
หัวหอมแดงหั่น	1 ช้อนโต๊ะ
พริกสดหั่น	2-3 เม็ด
มะนาว	1 ซีก
ต้นหอม	

วิธีทำ

ผ่าไข่เค็มใช้ช้อนตักเอาแต่ไข่แดง หรือ
ติดไข่ขาวเล็กน้อยหั่นเป็นชิ้นเล็ก ๆ จัด
ใส่จานโรยหน้าด้วยหอมแดง พริกและ
ต้นหอมหั่นวางมะนาวไว้ข้างๆ เวลารับ -
ประทานบีบมะนาวโรยให้ทั่วๆ.

CHICKEN CURRY (GREEN)

INGREDIENTS:

- 1 cup sliced chicken breasts
- 2 cups coconut milk or light cream
- 2 tablespoons green curry paste (see page 13)
- 1 cup sweet peas (frozen)
- 2 green chilies cut lengthwise
- 2 tablespoons nampla (fish sauce)
- 2 tablespoons vegetable oil

METHOD:

In a sauce pan heat oil over medium
heat. Stir—fry green curry paste for
1 minute. Add chicken and nampla.
Stir—fry until chicken is done. Add
coconut milk and bring to boil. Add
sweet peas and green chili. Stir a
few times. Remove from heat.

SALTY EGG SALAD

INGREDIENTS:

- 3 salty eggs (use only the yolks) (see page 19.)
- 1 tablespoon sliced red onions
- 1 tablespoon chopped hot pepper
- 1 piece lemon

METHOD:

Cut the salty eggs into small pieces.
On a serving plate layer egg, sliced
red onion, and hot chili ; top with
chopped spring onions and a wedge
of lemon. (Squeeze lemon before
eating).

Masman beef curry

In this picture three dishes are shown: the Masman Beef Curry in front center, the Stuffed Omelet on the top left and Indian Style Salad on the right.

After arriving in Jakarta we found that the last dish is also an Indonesian national dish called "Gado-Gado". There is only one minor difference, all vegetables in "Gado-Gado" are boiled, whereas in my version some are fresh. I guess a more proper name could then be Indonesian Style Salad. The Stuffed Omelet is a famour Thai dish of long standing. In Thailand the Masman Beef Curry is cooked with pineapple instead of apple.

แกงมัสมั่นเนื้อ

ส่วน

เนื้อสตู 2 ปอนด์		(1 กิโล)
กะทิ	3	ถ้วย
มันฝรั่งหัวเล็กๆ	5-6	หัว
หัวหอม 1 หัวหั่นเป็น 4 ชิ้น	2	หัว
แอ็ปเปิ้ลหั่น 2 ผล	(เขียว 1 แดง 1)	
เครื่องแกงมัสมั่น (2 ห่อ)	3	ช้อนโต๊ะ
	(ดูวิธีทำหน้า 14.)	
น้ำมะนาว	1	ช้อนชา
น้ำปลา	3	ช้อนโต๊ะ
น้ำตาล	1	ช้อนโต๊ะ
ถั่วลิสง	$\frac{1}{2}$	ถ้วย
น้ำมัน	$\frac{1}{2}$	ถ้วย

วิธีทำ

ตั้งกะทะใส่น้ำมันทอดเนื้อ พอเนื้อข้าง
นอกสุกเทใส่หม้อเติมกะทิ ตั้งพอน้ำกะทิ
เดือดปิดฝา เคี่ยวด้วยไฟอ่อนทิ้งไว้
ประมาณ 2 ชั่วโมงจนเนื้อเปื่อย ตักน้ำ
กะทิใส่กะทะสักครึ่งถ้วย ผัดเครื่องแกง
จนหอม เทใส่หม้อผสมกับเนื้อและกะทิ
เติมน้ำปลา น้ำตาล ชิมดูให้มีรสจัดใส่
ผักมันฝรั่งและหัวหอม และถั่วลิสงเคี่ยว
ต่อไปอีก 20 นาที ไฟกลางค่อนข้างอ่อน
พอมันสุกใส่แอปเปิ้ล ถ้าไม่มีรสเปรี้ยว
เติมน้ำมะนาวพอเดือดยกลง

MASMAN CURRY BEEF

INGREDIENTS:

   2 pounds (1 kilo) Stewing beef
   3 cups coconut milk
5−7 small potatoes
   2 onions cut in four pieces
   3 tablespoons masman curry
      paste (2 packages see page14)
   1 Teaspoon lemon juice
   3 tablespoons nampla
              (fish sauce)
   1 tablespoon sugar
   $\frac{1}{2}$ cup shelled peanuts
   $\frac{1}{2}$ cup vegetable oil
   1 red apple, sliced
   1 green apple, sliced

METHOD:

In a large saucepan, heat the oil,
add stewing beef. Cook until brown
(5 minutes). Add coconut milk and
bring to the boil. Lower the heat,
cover and let simmer for 2 hours
or until the meat is tender. Remove
$\frac{1}{2}$ cup of the liquid from the sauce
pan and put into a frying pan; mix
in curry paste and stir-fry for 2 minutes. Then pour curry paste mixture
into the meat mixture. Add nampla,
sugar, onions, potatoes and peanuts.
Cover and cook for 20 minutes more
on low heat. Add the 2 kinds of
apples. Remove from heat immediately.

ไข่ยัดไส้

ส่วน

หมูบด	½	ถ้วย
ถั่วแขกหั่นบางๆ	2	ช้อนโต๊ะ
มะเขือเทศหั่นเล็ก ๆ	1	ช้อนโต๊ะ
หัวหอมหั่นละเอียด	1	ช้อนโต๊ะ
หัวแครอทต้มแล้วหั่น	1	ช้อนโต๊ะ
เกลือกระเทียม	1	ช้อนชา
น้ำตาล	1	ช้อนชา
ซ๊อสแม๊กกี้ นิดหน่อย		พริกไทย
ไข่ 4 ฟอง		ผงชูรส
นม	1	ช้อนชา
น้ำมัน	½	ถ้วย

วิธีทำ

ใช้น้ำมันนิดหน่อยผัดหมูบด พอให้สุก
โรยผงเกลือกระเทียมผงชูรสใส่ผัก ถั่ว
แขก หัวหอม มะเขือเทศ แครอท ผัด
ต่อไปพอผักสุกใส่น้ำตาล ซ๊อสแม๊กกี้
โรยพริกไทยตักใส่ชามพักไว้ตีไข่กับน้ำ
นมเบา ๆ
ในกะทะใช้น้ำมันทากะทะให้ทั่ว เทไข่
ครึ่งหนึ่งลงในกะทะกรอกไข่ให้ไหลไป
บิดทั่วก้นกะทะ ตักไส้ครึ่งหนึ่งวางตรง
กลาง ใช้ตะหลิวพับไข่ให้เป็นสี่เหลี่ยม
ค่อย ๆ กลับให้ทางด้านพับลงกะทะเติม
น้ำมันทอดต่อไปจนเหลือง ทำอีกส่วน
ที่เหลือจะได้ไข่ยัดไส้สองอัน

STUFFED OMELET

INGREDIENTS:

- ½ cup ground pork
- 2 tablespoons green beans sliced thin
- 1 tablespoon chopped onion
- 1 tablespoon diced carrot (small dice)
- 1 teaspoon garlic salt
- 1 teaspoon sugar few drops maggie sauce dash of pepper
- 4 eggs
- 1 teaspoon milk
- ½ cup vegetable oil
- ¼ teaspoon monosodium glutamate (MSG.)

METHOD:

In a wok or saucepan heat 2 table-spoons of the oil. Add ground pork, sprinkle with garlic salt and MSG. Stir—fry for 3 minutes. Continue to cook; add green beans, onions and carrot, tossing lightly. Next add sugar, Maggie sauce and a dash of pepper. Remove from heat and pour into a bowl.

Beat eggs slightly with milk. Pour enough vegetable oil into a frying—pan to cover the bottom. Heat, pour in half of the egg mixture, rocking the pan to be sure egg is equal thickness. Put half of the ground pork mixture in the middle of the egg. Fold the egg omelet over the meat so that a square is formed.

Carefully turn over, cook for a few minutes. Remove to a serving plate, Makes two stuffed omelets.

สลัดแขก

ส่วน

ผักสลัด	½	หัว
มะเขือเทศผานบางๆ	1	ลูก
ถั่วงอก	½	ถ้วย
เต้าหู้ทอดหั่น	2	ช้อนโต๊ะ
ไข่ต้ม	1	ฟอง
มันฝรั่งทอด	½	ถ้วย
พริกป่น	1	ช้อนชา
หัวหอมสับละเอียด	1	ช้อนโต๊ะ
เนยถั่ว	1	ช้อนโต๊ะ
น้ำตาล	1	ช้อนโต๊ะ
น้ำปลา	1	ช้อนโต๊ะ
นมหรือกะทิ	½	ถ้วย
น้ำมันพืช	2	ช้อนโต๊ะ

วิธีทำ

น้ำสลัด ใช้น้ำมันพืชทอดหัวหอมสับ จนเหลือง เติมนมหรือกะทิ ลดไฟลงให้ อ่อน เติมพริกป่น เนยถั่ว น้ำตาล น้ำปลาชิมดูตามชอบ ให้มีรสเค็มหวาน ยกลงทิ้งไว้ให้เย็นต้มถั่วงอก พอสุกตัก ขึ้น ใส่กระชอนพักไว้ให้สะเด็ดน้ำ หั่น ผักสลัดให้เป็นชิ้นๆ 2"×2" ล้างสลัดให้ แห้ง จัดใส่ชามเรียงรอบด้วยมะเขือเทศ ถั่วงอกต้ม เต้าหู้ทอดไข่ต้มผ่าเป็น 4 ชิ้น ต่อ 1 ฟองราดหน้าด้วยน้ำสลัด โรยหน้า ด้วยมันฝรั่งทอด

INDIAN STYLE SALAD

INGREDIENTS:

½ head lettuce
1 tomato sliced thin
½ cup bean sprouts
2 tablespoons sliced bean curd
   cake (optional)
1 hard boiled egg
½ cup potato chips
6 sliced dried bean curd (see
   glossary)
1 teaspoon chili powder
1 tablespoon minced onion
2 tablespoons peanut butter
1 teaspoon sugar
1 tablespoon nampla
   (fish sauce)
½ cup milk or coconut milk
2 tablespoons vegetable oil

METHOD:

Heat the oil in a heavy sauce—pan, brown the minced onion, pour in milk and lower the heat. Add chili powder, peanut butter, sugar, nampla. Stir—mix until smooth. Remove from heat and set aside to cool. Boil the water and pour over the bean sprouts; drain. Cut and clean head lettuce and arrange on a serving plate. Layer with sliced tomato, cooked bean sprouts, sliced dried bean curd, and on top of all, the sliced hard boiled egg. Before serving pour the cooled dressing over the salad and top with potato chips.

Shrimp curry in pie shell

This dish has the Indian curry flavour that is wellknown throughout the world. The Thai word "Kari" is actually the Thai pronounciation of curry, whereas the other Thai word for curry is "Kang" as described earlier.

แกงกะหรี่กุ้งในแบ้งพาย

ส่วน

กุ้งปอกล้างผ่าหลัง	1 ถ้วย
หัวหอมหัวย่อมๆ ปอก	2 หัว
หัวหอมสับละเอียด	1 ช้อนโต๊ะ
ผงกะหรี่ 1 ช้อนโต๊ะ	เนย 2 ช้อนโต๊ะ
แบ้งสาลี 2 ช้อนโต๊ะ	เกลือ 1 ช้อนชา
มันฝรั่งต้ม 2 หัว	นมสด $\frac{1}{2}$ ถ้วย
หัวแครอทต้ม 1 หัว	พริก 2 เม็ด
ข้าวสุก 1 ถ้วย	สีเหลือง 2-3 หยด
แบ้งพายสำหรับ	1 ชิ้น
	(ดูวิธีทำข้างล่าง)

วิธีทำ

ละลายเนยในกะทะไฟอ่อนๆ พอเนย
ละลาย ใส่แบ้งสาลีทอดแบ้งจนเหลือง
ใส่กุ้ง หัวหอมสับ ผัดต่อไป ใส่ผงกะหรี่
ผัดต่อไป จนหัวหอมสุก เทใส่แบ้งพาย
เทข้าวสุกใส่ชาม หยดสีเหลืองลงไป
เคล้าให้เข้ากันใส่พิมพ์กดให้เป็นถ้วยวาง
ถ้วยตรงกลางแกงกะหรี่กุ้งในแบ้งพาย.

แบ้งพาย

ส่วน

แบ้งสาลี 1 ถ้วย	เกลือ $\frac{1}{4}$ ช้อนชา
น้ำเย็น 2 ช้อนโต๊ะ	ไขมันพืช $\frac{1}{2}$ ถ้วย

วิธีทำ

ร่อนแบ้งกับเกลือ แล้วผสมลงด้วยไขมัน
พืช ใช้มีดตัดแบ้งให้เป็นเม็ดเล็กๆ เท่า
เม็ดถั่วลันเตา เติมน้ำนวดเบาๆ ให้เข้า
กัน คลึงแบ้งให้บางวางลงในจานพาย
เส้นผ่าศูนย์กลาง 9'' ตกแต่งริมแบ้ง อบ
ไฟ 375° ประมาณ 20 นาที.

SHRIMP CURRY IN PIE SHELL

INGREDIENTS:

- 1 cup shelled and cleaned shrimp
- 2 small white onions pealed
- 1 tablespoon minced onion
- 1 tablespoon curry powder
- 1 tablespoon butter
- 2 tablespoons flour
- $\frac{1}{2}$ cup milk 2 potatoes boiled
- 1 carrot boiled and cut into 1'' segments
- 2 chili peppers cut into 1'' segments 1 cup cooked rice
- 2–3 drops yellow food coloring
- 1 pie crust shell

METHOD:

Melt butter on very low heat, stir in flour until light brown. Add the shrimp, minced onion and stir—fry on medium heat for 2 minutes. Add curry powder, salt, and milk; stir until thickened. Add onions, potatoes, carrot and chili pepper. Cook for 3 minutes. Pour into cooked pie shell. Drop food coloring on the cooked rice and mix well. Place into a small wet mold, press and place on top of the shrimp curry in pie shell. Serve.

PIE CRUST: 1 cup sifted flour
$\frac{1}{2}$ cup shortening $\frac{1}{2}$ teaspoon salt
2 tablespoons cold water

Sift together the flour and salt. Cut in shortening with pastry blender or blending fork, until pieces are the size of small peas. Sprinkle water over mixture. Gently toss with fork and form into a ball. On lightly to floured board roll out gently until a circle is formed in $\frac{1}{8}$ inch thick. Place on 9'' pie plate. Fold overhang under; make edging as shown above Bake in oven 375 degrees for 20 minutes.

Sour and hot curry

The hot and sour curry is a real Thai farmer's invention. This curry does not have coconut milk because it is planned to be cooked fast. It is most suitable for a farmer who has left for work early and come· home hungry and requires quick hot meal with the fish that he may picked up from the canal on the way home. It has become a favorite with the city people as well, because of its fine sharp taste.

แกงส้ม

ส่วน

กุ้งปอกล้างผ่าหลัง	½ ถ้วย
น้ำพริกแกงส้ม	1 ห่อ
	(ดูหน้า 11)
น้ำส้มมะขามหรือน้ำมะนาว	2 ช้อนโต๊ะ
น้ำปลา	2 ช้อนโต๊ะ
น้ำตาล	1 ช้อนโต๊ะ
ผักหั่น (กะหล่ำปลี, สค้วอช, ดอกกะหล่ำ)	
	2 ถ้วย
น้ำ	1½ ถ้วย

วิธีทำ

ต้มกุ้งพอสุกในน้ำ 1½ ถ้วย ตักเนื้อกุ้งตำ
ให้ละเอียดเติมน้ำพริกแกงส้มตำต่อไป
จนเข้าเนื้อกันดี ละลายในน้ำ ต้มกุ้ง ตั้ง
ไฟให้เดือด เติมน้ำปลา น้ำตาล มะนาว
(หรือน้ำส้มมะขาม) ชิมตามชอบ ใส่ผัก
ต้มต่อไปจนผักสุกยกลง

หมายเหตุ

ถ้าเติมปลาร้าบ่นโอชาของพันท้ายนร-
สิงห์ 1 ช้อนชา จะเพิ่มรสให้แหลมอร่อย
ขึ้นมาก.

HOT AND SOUR CURRY

INGREDIENTS:

- ½ cup shelled cleaned shrimp
- 1 package or 2 tablespoons of Kang Som paste (see page 11)
- 2 tablespoons tamarind juice (or lemon juice see glossary)
- 2 tablespoons nampla (fish sauce)
- 1 tablespoon sugar
- 2 cups squash sliced (may use cauliflower, cabbage etc.)
- 1½ cups water

METHOD:

Cook the shrimp in 1½ cups water until done (approximately 10 minutes). Remove shrimp, saving the broth. Pound the shrimp in a mortar together with the Kang Som paste, and add to the broth. Cook over medium heat. Season with nampla, sugar, tamarind or lemon juice. Add the squash. Cover for 5 minutes and simmer. Remove from heat.

ไข่กวนหมู

ส่วน

ไข่	2	ฟอง
นมสด	1	ช้อนชา
หมูบด	2	ช้อนโต๊ะ
ผงเกลือกระเทียม	$\frac{1}{4}$	ช้อนชา
น้ำปลา	1	ช้อนชา
หัวหอมสับ	1	ช้อนโต๊ะ
น้ำมันพืช	$\frac{1}{2}$	ถ้วย

วิธีทำ

ตีไข่เบา ๆ ด้วยปลายซ่อมผสมด้วยน้ำนม และน้ำปลาพักไว้ เคล้าหมูบดกับหอมสับ ผงกระเทียมเกลือให้เข้ากันใส่ในไข่ที่ตีไว้ ตั้งกะทะเล็กก้นแบน เส้นผ่าศูนย์กลาง 6" เทน้ำมันลงไปพอร้อนใส่ส่วนผสมไข่หรี่ไฟลงให้อ่อนทอดสัก 3 นาที พลิกทอดอีกข้างทอดต่อไปจนสุกตักใส่จานเสริฟร้อน ๆ.

INGREDIENTS :

   2 eggs
   1 teaspoon milk
   2 tablespoons ground pork
   $\frac{1}{2}$ teaspoon garlic salt
   1 teaspoon nampla (fish sauce)
   1 tablespoon chopped onion
   $\frac{1}{2}$ cup vegetable oil

METHOD :

Beat the eggs lightly with a fork. Add milk, nampla, and continue beating until well mixed. Combine ground pork, garlic salt, chopped onion, and stir into the egg mixture. Heat the oil in a 6 inch frying pan on medium heat; when hot, pour in the egg mixture, lower the heat and cook for 3 minutes. Carefully turn over to the other side and cook for 3 minutes more. Remove to the serving plate. Serve hot.

ยำไทย

ส่วน

ผักกาดหอมหั่น	$\frac{1}{2}$ ถ้วย
แครอทขูดเป็นชิ้นๆ ทำเป็นวงๆ แช่น้ำ	1 หัว
หอมแดงหั่นเป็นวงๆ	1 หัว
กุ้งตัวงามๆ ต้มผ่าเป็นสอง	3 ตัว
หมูหั่นเป็นชิ้น 2"x1" (ต้ม)	2 ช้อนโต๊ะ
ไข่ต้ม	1 ฟอง
น้ำตาล	2 ช้อนโต๊ะ
เกลือ	1 ช้อนชา
น้ำส้ม	1 ช้อนโต๊ะ
น้ำ	1 ช้อนโต๊ะ
พริกบ่น	$\frac{1}{2}$ ช้อนชา

วิธีทำ

หั่นผักต่างๆ แช่น้ำเย็นทิ้งไว้ 15 นาที ใส่กระชอนทิ้งไว้ให้สะเด็ดน้ำ ต้มกุ้ง ปอกผ่าเป็นสองซีก หั่นหมูต้ม หั่นไข่ ต้มพักไว้ ใช้หม้อเล็กๆ เคี่ยวน้ำตาล เกลือพอเหนียวยกลง เติมน้ำส้มและ พริกบ่นคนให้เข้ากัน เทผักใส่ชาม พร้อมทั้งหมูและกุ้งราดด้วยน้ำส้มน้ำตาล ที่ผสมไว้เคล้าให้เข้ากัน ใส่จานเสริฟ เรียงหมูกุ้งไว้บนและวางไข่ต้มไว้บนสุด เสริฟทันที.

THAI STYLE SALAD

INGREDIENTS :

$\frac{1}{2}$ cup cut up head lettuce
1 carrot, peeled, sliced lengthwise and curled
1 medium red onion sliced
3 medium shrimp
2 tablespoons chopped cooked pork
1 hard boiled egg sliced
2 tablespoons sugar
1 tablespoon vinegar
1 teaspoon salt
1 tablespoon water
$\frac{1}{2}$ tablespoon chili powder.

METHOD :

Cut all the vegetables. Soak in cold water for 15 minutes. Drain.

Boil the shrimp, peel, cut lengthwise in two. In a small sauce−pan cook the sugar, vinegar and salt until syrup. Add the chili powder stir well. Cool. In a salad (mixing) bowl, combine lettuce, carrots, onion, pork and shrimp. Add the vinegar mixture tossing lightly with salad fork. Arrange on a serving plate, top with sliced hard boiled egg, and serve.

Steamed fish a la Bangkok

The basic Thai method calls for banana leaf cup to be used as a container. It is quite difficult to find banana leaves in the States so I have tried artichokes and found them quite acceptable. You can also eat the artichoke leaf whereas you cannot do so with banana leaf. You can use heat resistant containers in place of artichokes.

ห่อหมกปลา

ส่วน

ปลาแล่เป็นชิ้นบางๆ	1	ถ้วย
น้ำพริกแกงแดง	2	ช้อนโต๊ะ
น้ำปลา	2	ช้อนโต๊ะ
ใบโหระพาใบกะหล่ำปลีหั่น	1	ถ้วย
หัวกระทิสด	1½	ถ้วย
ไข่	1	ฟอง
ใบมะกรูดหั่นฝอยหรือใบหอมหั่น		
	1	ช้อนโต๊ะ
พริกแดงปาดเป็นเส้นเล็กๆ	1	เม็ด

วิธีทำ

นำน้ำพริก หัวกะทิ ปลาแล่เป็นชิ้น
บางๆ ลงในชาม คนด้วยไม้พายจนเข้า
กันดี เติมน้ำปลาและไข่คนต่อไปจน
เข้ากันดี เทใส่กระทงซึ่งรองด้วยใบ
กะหล่ำปลีและใบโหระพา โรยหน้าด้วย
ใบมะกรูดหรือใบหอมฝอยวางพริกแดง
เป็นกากะบาดนึ่งในรังถึงไฟร้อนจัดประ
มาณ 30 - 35 นาที.

หมายเหตุ

ถ้าทำในต่างประเทศใบตองมักหายากจะ
ใช้ หัวอาทิโชกแทนกระทงก็ได้ ใช้
หัวอาทิโชก 5 หัว ต้มคว่ำหน้าลงในน้ำ
เดือดประมาณ 3-5 นาที นำมาดึงไส้
กลางออกใช้กรรไกรขลิบปลาย แต่งให้
สวยงามรองก้นด้วยกะหล่ำปลี เทส่วน
ผสมปลาและกะทิลง อย่าให้เต็มมากนัก
ตบแต่งด้วยใบหอมและพริกแดง.

STEAMED FISH CURRY A LA BANGKOK

INGREDIENTS :

- 1 pound ($\frac{1}{2}$ kilo) of fish
- 2 tablespoons red curry paste (see page 12)
- 1 tablespoon nampla (fish sauce)
- 1 cup chopped cabbage or sweet basil leaves
- 1½ cups coconut thick milk
- 1 egg
- 1 tablespoon chopped green onion
- 1 red chili cut into pieces
- 5 artichokes

METHOD :

To boil artichokes : Strip off large outside leaves. Cut off stalks and trim base neatly. Rub with lemon to prevent turning black. Snip off the top of each leaf with kitchen scissors within about one inch of the base. Remove the inner choke. Blanch head-down in fast boiling water. Let boil for 3—5 minutes. Drain and cool.

Cut fish into thin slices. Put fish into a bowl, add nampla, coconut milk, and curry paste, stirring with a wooden spoon. Add egg, and stir until mixture become thick. Put some cabbage or sweet basil on the bottom of artichokes. Spoon the fish mixture into the artichokes. Sprinkle top with chopped green onion and cut red chili. Steam for 30—35 minutes. Serve hot or cold.

Fried shrimp with chili sauce

This is an ideal food to take to a pot luck: it carries easily without spilling and those who do not care for the spicy chili sauce can take the shrimp by itself.

กุ้งทอดราดพริก

ส่วน

กุ้งตัวงาม 5-6 ตัว	(½ กิโล)
น้ำพริกแกงแดง	1 ห่อ
	(ดูหน้า 13.)
กุ้งแห้ง	2 ช้อนโต๊ะ
น้ำปลา	1 ช้อนโต๊ะ
น้ำตาล	1 ช้อนโต๊ะ
เกลือผงกระเทียม	½ ช้อนชา

ใบมะกรูดหั่นฝอย (หรือใบหอม) นิด-
หน่อย

ผงชูรส

วิธีทำ

ปอกกุ้งเหลือหางไว้ ผ่าหลังชักเส้นดำ
ล้าง โรยด้วย เกลือ ผงกะเทียมและผง
ชูรสหมักทิ้งไว้ 10-15 นาที แล้วนำไป
ทอดไฟกลาง ๆ พอสุกตักกุ้งเรียงใส่จาน
ไว้น้ำมันที่เหลือหรี่ไฟลงอ่อน ๆ ผัดน้ำ
พริกพอหอมเดิมน้ำตาลน้ำปลาและกุ้ง
แห้งผัดจนเข้าเนื้อกัน เทน้ำพริกราดบน
ตัวกุ้งโรยด้วยใบมะกรูด หรือใบหอมรับ
ประทานกับข้าว.

FRIED SHRIMP WITH CHILI SAUCE

INGREDIENTS :
  6 large shrimp
  1 tablespoon red curry paste
    (See page 13)
  2 tablespoons pounded dried
    shrimp.
  1 tablespoon nampla (fish sauce)
  1 tablespoon sugar
  ½ teaspoon garlic salt
  ½ cup vegetable oil
  1 teaspoon chopped green onion
  Dash Monosodium glutamate
  (MSG)

METHOD :
Shell and clean the shrimp; rub
with MSG. garlic salt and set aside
for 15 minutes.
Heat the oil in a large frypan over
medium heat. When hot, fry the
shrimp approximately 2½ minutes
on each side. Remove to serving
plate. Using the left over oil and
low heat, stir-fry curry paste for 1
minute, season with sugar and
nampla, add dried shrimp and stir-
fry for 1 minute more. Pour the
cooked paste over the fried shrimp.
Garnish with chopped green onions.
Serve with rice.

Green vegetables
and chicken in peanut sauce

In Bangkok, we use morning glory vine as the basic vegetable but spinach tastes well with the preparation. This is a quick lunch idea which is not very fattening. Few Thai restaurants serve this, but it is considered quite exclusive dish in the old Thai menu. Often meat is used instead of chicken.

พระรามลงสรงไก่

ส่วน

เนื้อไก่อกกล้วนๆ หั่นเป็นชิ้น 1 ถ้วย
กระเทียม   2 กลีบ
ผงกะหรี่   1 ช้อนชา
นม 1 ช้อนโต๊ะ เนย 1 ช้อนโต๊ะ
ผักโขมจีนหั่น   1 ช้อนโต๊ะ
ต้นหอมหั่นเป็นท่อนยาว-2" ½ ถ้วย
หอมแดงสับละเอียด   1 ช้อนโต๊ะ
พริกบ่น 1 ช้อนชา   ขิง 1 แว่น
เนยถั่ว   2 ช้อนโต๊ะ
น้ำตาล   1 ช้อนโต๊ะ
น้ำปลา   1 ช้อนชา
กะทิหรือนมสด   ½ ถ้วย
น้ำพริกเผา (ดูหน้า 11) 1 ช้อนชา
น้ำมันพืช   2 ช้อนโต๊ะ

วิธีทำ

ตำขิงและกระเทียมเข้าด้วยกันให้ละเอียด
แล้วเคล้ากับเนื้อไก่เติมผงกะหรี่ เนย
นม หมักทิ้งไว้ 1 ชม.

ในกะทะใช้น้ำมัน 2 ช้อนโต๊ะ   ไฟ
กลาง ๆ ทอดหอมสับจนเหลืองหรี่ไฟใส่
พริกบ่นผัดต่อไปใส่เนยถั่ว น้ำตาล น้ำ-
ปลา   และกะทิหรือนมสดคนให้เข้ากัน
ดียกลง
ต้มผักโขมและต้นหอม พอสุก ตักให้
สะเด็ดน้ำจัดใส่จานเสริฟรวนไก่ในกะทะ
ไม่ต้องใช้น้ำมันพอสุก เทลงบนผักราด
ด้วยน้ำพริกที่ผสมกับเนยถั่ว หยอดน้ำ
พริกเผาไว้ตรงกลาง รับประทานกับข้าว
ก็ได้หรือจะทานเปล่าๆ ก็ได้สำหรับ 2 คน

GREEN VEGETABLES, CHICKEN IN PEANUT SAUCE

INGREDIENTS:

1 cup sliced chicken breast
1 slice ginger root
2 cloves garlic
1 teaspoon curry powder
1 tablespoon butter
1 tablespoon light cream or eva-
    porated milk
1½ cups cut spinach
1½ cups cut spring onion
    (2'' pieces including top)
1 tablespoon minced red onion
1 tablespoon chili powder
2 tablespoons peanut butter
1 tablespoon sugar
1 teaspoon nampla (fish sauce)
½ cup milk or coconut milk
1 teaspoon roasted curry paste
    (see page 11)
2 tablespoons vegetable oil

METHOD:

Pound ginger root together with garlic, curry powder. cream and melted
butter.   Pour over chicken breasts
and marinate for 1 hour.

Heat the oil in a heavy saucepan
over medium heat.   Brown minced
onion until golden brown. Lower
the heat, add peanut butter, sugar,
nampla, chili powder and milk. Stir-
fry for 1 minute. Remove from heat.
In boiling water cook spinach and
spring onion for 3 minutes.   Drain.
place on serving plate. Brown the
chicken breast in a saucepan (without oil) turning until done. Remove
from heat and place on top of
cooked spinach and spring onion.
Pour the peanut sauce over the chi
cken and top with roasted curry
paste. Serve.

Pot roast beef

The following three dishes make a good combination for picnic basket because they can be prepared ahead of time and will taste equally well hot or cold. Bring along a lot of rice because all Thai food has a strong taste that needs to be neutralized by rice. The Thai style container in the picture may not be easy to get, but any food container will do.

เนื้ออบ

ส่วน

เนื้อสำหรับทำสตู	½ กิโล
กระเทียมสับ	1 ช้อนชา
ขิง	1 แว่น
ซีอิ๊ว (คิโคแมน)	2 ช้อนโต๊ะ
น้ำตาล	1 ช้อนโต๊ะ
เกลือ	1 ช้อนชา
มันฝรั่งปอกผ่าสี่	2 หัว
ถั่วแขกหั่นเป็น 2 ท่อน	½ ถ้วย
น้ำมัน	2 ช้อนโต๊ะ
น้ำ	1 ถ้วย

วิธีทำ

เคล้าเนื้อกับกระเทียมพริกไทย เกลือ ทิ้งไว้ 1 ชม. ตั้งกะทะพอไฟร้อนใส่ น้ำมันทอดเนื้อที่หมักไว้พอสุกใส่น้ำตาล ซีอิ๊ว ผัดต่อไปใส่น้ำพอเดือดใส่ขิงปิด ฝาลดไฟให้อ่อนเคี่ยวทิ้งประมาณ 1 ชม. หรือจนเนื้อเปื่อย ใส่มันและถั่วปิดฝา เคี่ยวต่อไปอีก 20 นาทียกลง.

POT ROAST BEEF

INGREDIENTS:

  1 pound stewing beef
  1 teaspoon minced garlic
  ½ teaspoon pepper
  1 piece ginger root
  2 tablespoons soy sauce
  1 tablespoon sugar
  1 teaspoon salt
  2 medium potatoes (peel, cut in fourths)
  ½ cup green beans (cut in two)
  1 cup water

METHOD:

Rub the meat with salt, pepper and minced garlic and let stand for 1 hour. Heat the oil in a heavy saucepen, add the meat turning over a few times. Add sugar, soy sauce and water. Adjust seasoning, add ginger, and bring to the boil. Cover, reduce heat to very low, and simmer for 1 hour until the meat is tender. Add the potato and green beans. Cover and simmer for 20 minutes more. Remove and arrange on serving plate.

พะโล้บึกไก่

ส่วน

ไข่ต้มปอกเปลือก	10	ฟอง
บึกไก่	½	กิโล
กระเทียมสับ	1	ช้อนชา
ผักชีสับ	1	ช้อนชา
พริกไทย	½	ช้อนชา
อบเชยผง	¼	ช้อนชา
น้ำตาลอ้อย	2	ช้อนโต๊ะ
เกลือ	1	ช้อนชา
น้ำ	2	ถ้วย
น้ำมันพืช	2	ช้อนโต๊ะ

วิธีทำ

ตั้งกะทะใส่น้ำมันพอร้อนใส่กระเทียมสับ
และผักชีสับพริกไทยผัดจนหอมใส่บึกไก่
กลับไปมาจนทั่ว ใส่ซีอิ๊ว น้ำตาล เกลือ
กลับไปมาจนบึกไก่เป็นสีน้ำตาล เทใส่
หม้อเติมน้ำใส่ไข่ต้ม โรยด้วยอบเชยบ่น
พอเดือดบิดฝาลดไฟเคี่ยวต่อไปประมาณ
1 ชั่วโมง.

EGGS AND CHICKEN WINGS
IN BROWN SAUCE

INGREDIENTS:

    10 eggs (hard boiled)
    1 pound chicken wings
    1 teaspoon minced garlic
    1 teaspoon minced coriander
    ½ teaspoon pepper
    ¼ teaspoon cinnamon
    2 tablespoons brown sugar
    1 teaspoon salt
    1 quart water
    2 tablespoons vegetable oil

METHOD:

Hard boil the eggs, soak in cold
water, peel and set aside. Heat
the oil in A large frying pan, brown
the minced garlic until light brown,
add the minced coriander, pepper
and stir—fry constantly. Add chicken
wings, turning over a few times;
add brown sugar, soy sauce, nampla and continue turning.   Place
the chicken in a large pot, add the
water and bring to the boil; add
the hard boiled eggs.   Lower the
heat. Cover. Let simmer for 1
hour.

เต้าเจี้ยวหลน

ส่วน

เต้าเจี้ยว	½ ถ้วย
หัวหอมหั่น	2 ช้อนโต๊ะ
พริกสด	3 เม็ด
หมูบด	2 ช้อนโต๊ะ
กะทิสด	1 ถ้วย
น้ำตาล	1 ช้อนชา
น้ำปลา	1 ช้อนชา

ผักสด เช่น ต้นหอม แตงกวา
กะหล่ำปลี

วิธีทำ

ตั้งกะทิเคี่ยวจนแตกมัน ใส่เต้าเจี้ยวคน
ให้เข้ากันใส่หอมหั่นและหมูสับ คนอย่า
ให้หมูเป็นก้อนพอหมูสุกเติมน้ำตาล น้ำ
ปลา พริกสด พอพริกสุกยกลงรับประ-
ทานกับผักสด.

BROWN BEAN SAUCE DIP

INGREDIENTS:

½ cup brown bean sauce

(see glossary)

2 tablespoons chopped red onion

3 chili peppers

2 tablespoons ground pork

1 cup coconut milk

1 teaspoon sugar

1 teaspoon nampla (fish sauce)

spring onions, cucumber, cabbage.

METHOD:

Heat the coconut milk and bring to the boil; add brown bean sauce, chopped red onion, and stir well. Stir in ground pork. Add sugar, nampla and chili pepper. Simmer for 5 minutes, and spoon into a bowl. Serve with spring onions, cucumber and cabbage.

Hot shrimp dip

We often received comments from readers and book reviewers that the title of <u>Cooking Thai Food In American Kitchens</u> turned them off. My only answer is that America is my favorite place and American kitchens, I like most. I hope our many friends in the Washington, D.C. area will be reminded of their days in Thailand by this book.

Somehow, the shrimp dip which comes from the Northeast of Thailand is just as appropriate in America when a hot spicy dip is desired.

น้ำพริกปลาร้ากุ้งสด

ส่วน

กุ้งปอกล้างชักเส้นดำ	½	ถ้วย
พริกสด	5-7	เม็ด
หัวหอมแดงหั่น	2	ช้อนโต๊ะ
กระเทียม	5	กลีบ
เกลือ	1	ช้อนชา
น้ำปลา	1	ช้อนโต๊ะ
น้ำมะนาว	1	ช้อนโต๊ะ
น้ำสุก (ต้มกุ้ง)	2	ช้อนโต๊ะ
ผงชูรส	½	ช้อนชา

ผัก สำหรับจิ้ม กระหล่ำปลี, กระเจี๊ยบ, แอสปารากัส, บรัสเซิลสเปร้า, แตงกวา

วิธีทำ

ต้มกุ้งให้สุก (ใส่น้ำพอท่วมกุ้ง) พักไว้ให้เย็น ใช้กระดาษตะกั่วห่อพริกกระ – เทียมหอมแล้วย่างบนไฟ ข้างละ 2 นาที ใส่ครกตำพอละเอียดไม่มาก ใส่กุ้งต้มตำต่อไป จนเข้าเนื้อกันดีแล้วตักใส่ชาม เติมน้ำต้มกุ้งสัก 2 ช้อนโต๊ะปรุงด้วยผงชูรส เกลือ น้ำปลา น้ำมะนาว ใช้ช้อนคนให้เข้ากัน ผ่ากะหล่ำปลีหัวหนึ่งเบนสี่ชิ้นต้มพอสุกอย่าให้สุกมาก ตัก-ขึ้นพักไว้ ต้มกระเจี๊ยบ แอสปารากัส-บรัสเซิลสเปร้า แล้วเรียงใส่จานไว้กับแตงกวาสด (ปอกหั่นไว้แล้ว) จัดน้ำพริกกุ้งไว้ตรงกลาง รับประทานกับข้าวร้อนๆ.

HOT SHRIMP DIP

INGREDIENTS:

½ cup shelled, cleaned shrimp
5–7 chili peppers
2 tablespoons chopped red onion
5 cloves garlic
1 teaspoon salt
1 tablespoon nampla (fish s auce)
2 tablespoons shrimp broth
½ teaspoon monosodium glutamate (MSG) (optional)
1 tablespoon lemon juice
cabbage, okra, asparagus,
brussels sprouts or other vegetables for dipping.

METHOD:

In a small sauce pan cook the shrimp and save the broth.
Wrap chili peppers, garlic and onion with aluminum foil. Roast on me-dium low heat for 2 minutes on each side; unwrap, place in mortar, and pound until fine. Add the shrimp and pound until well mixed. Add 2 tablespoons shrimp broth-Season with MSG, nampla, salt and lemon juice. Spoon onto the serving dish. Trim all the vegetables, wash, and drain. Cook uncovered in boiling water for 5 minutes. Drain. arrange on the serving plate. Put the shrimp dip dish in the center. Serve.

Boat trip chili paste salad

It is not easy to find this dish in a Thai restaurant. The dish originated from the Royal palace Kitchen quite a few years ago. It is still considered a very exclusive dish with a lot of care put into the preparation and the arrangement of vegetable and other ingredients. Westeners will find the dish quite agreeable because of the taste of sweet pork.

น้ำพริกลงเรือ

ส่วน

พริกสดเด็ดก้าน	7	เม็ด
กระเทียม	3	กลีบ
กะปิ	1	ช้อนโต๊ะ
กุ้งแห้งบ่น	2	ช้อนโต๊ะ
น้ำมะนาว	2	ช้อนโต๊ะ
น้ำปลา	1	ช้อนโต๊ะ
น้ำตาลบีก	1	ช้อนโต๊ะ
ไข่เค็มใช้เฉพาะไข่แดง	1	ฟอง

ปลากรอบทอด 1 ชิ้นหรือกุ้งแห้งทอด
1 ช้อนโต๊ะ

น้ำมันพืช	1	ถ้วย
หมูหวาน	½	ถ้วย

ผัก มะเขือ แตงกวา และอื่นๆ ตามชอบ

วิธีทำ

ผ่ามะเขือลูกหนึ่งเป็น 4 ชิ้นแกะเม็ดออก
ปอกแตงกวาหั่นเป็นชิ้นพอคำแช่ในน้ำ-
มะนาว เทใส่กะชอนให้สะเด็ดน้ำจัดใส่
จาน ตำพริกสด กับกระเทียม ให้ละ
เอียดพอสมควร เติมกะปิตำต่อไป ใส่มะ
นาว น้ำปลา น้ำตาล กุ้งแห้งบ่น ชิมดู
ตามชอบ ใช้น้ำมัน 2 ช้อนโต๊ะตั้งไฟ
อ่อนๆ ผัดน้ำพริกให้สุกทิ้งไว้ให้เย็น
แล้วราดน้ำพริกลงบนผัก แต่งหน้าด้วย
ปลากรอบทอด หรือกุ้งแห้งทอดไข่เค็ม
และหมูหวาน รับประทานกับข้าว.

BOAT TRIP CHILI SHRIMP
PASTE SALAD

INGREDIENTS:

2 tablespoons dried shrimp
7 hot chilies
3 cloves garlic
1 tablespoon shrimp paste
(kapi)
1 tablespoon nampla
(fish sauce)
1 tablespoon sugar
2 tablespoons lemon juice
1 salty egg yolk (see page.19)
1 piece of fried dried fish (pla-grob) see glossary.
1 cup vegetable oil
½ cup of sweet pork
(see page 19 for sweet pork)
2 cups cut eggplant, cucumber, radish or any kind of vegetable you like

METHOD:

Pound dried shrimp. Add garlic
and crush coarsely. Add shrimp
paste, chilies; pound together until
it becomes a paste. Season to
taste with nampla, sugar and lemon
juice. Heat two tablespoons vegetable oil. Fry the chilies and
shrimp paste mixture on low heat
until brown.
Cut cucumber, eggplant, radish,
into small pieces and place in
serving dish. Top with fried shrimp
paste. Sprinkle with chopped salty
egg, fried fish and sweet pork. Serve
with rice.

Ground pork chili dip

This famous northern dish is quite spicy, which is why it is always taken with fresh vegetables. It is a characteristic of northern cooking to add pork to most of their dishes For a northener, this dish would be taken with glutinous rice. It is equally tasty with boiled rice. The pork rind is a "must" item in the ingredients.

น้ำพริกอ่อง

ส่วน

น้ำพริกแกงส้ม	1	ช้อนโต๊ะ
		(1 ห่อ)
กระเทียมสับ	1	ช้อนชา
มะเขือเทศสีดา	7	ผล
หมูสับ	½	ถ้วย
น้ำตาล	1	ช้อนชา
น้ำปลา	2	ช้อนโต๊ะ
แค็บหมู	1	ถ้วย

ผักสด, แตงกวา, กะหล่ำปลี, ดอก
กะหล่ำ

วิธีทำ

ผ่ามะเขือเทศเอาเม็ดออก ตำเข้าด้วยกัน
กับน้ำพริกแกงส้ม เจียวกระเทียมจน
หอมผัดน้ำพริกแกงส้ม ผัดพอละลาย
ใส่หมูปรุงรสด้วยน้ำตาล น้ำปลา พอ
หมูสุกตักใส่ชามเสริฟรับประทานกับผัก
สดเช่น แตงกวา, กะหล่ำปลี และ
ดอกกะหล่ำ และแค็บหมู.

GROUND PORK HOT DIP

INGREDIENTS:
1 tablespoon or 1 package
   Kang Som paste (see page 11)
1 teaspoon minced garlic
7 cherry tomatoes
½ cup ground pork
1 teaspoon sugar
2 tablespoons nampla (fish
   sauce)
1 cup fried pork rind (canned)
cucumber, cabbage, cauliflower,
etc.

METHOD:
Clean, cut and seed cherry tomatoes.
Put into a mortar and pound with
Kang Som paste until smooth.

In a saucepan warm oil over medium
heat. Brown garlic until light brown.
Add paste and stir—fry until blended.
Add ground pork, sugar and nampla.
Keep on stirring until the pork is
cooked. Spoon into a serving dish.
Serve with pork rind and your favo-
rite vegetables.

Pineapple Fried rice

For a beautiful party idea, this dish should be served in a fresh hollow pineapple. I have found that it is not very easy to find fresh pineapple in any supermarket in the US. You may have to use canned pineapple in the ingredients, be sure to drain all the syrup out first. If you can find fresh pineapple. Use fresh meat to dice and the hollow pineapple to serve the dish.

ข้าวผัดสับปะรด

ส่วน

ข้าวสุก	3 ถ้วย
สับปะรดสดหั่นเป็น 4 เหลี่ยมเล็กๆ $\frac{1}{2}$ ถ้วย	
ขนมบังหั่น 4 เหลี่ยมเล็กๆ $\frac{1}{2}$ ถ้วย	
หัวหอมหั่น 4 เหลี่ยมเล็กๆ 2 ช้อนโต๊ะ	
ผงชูรส $\frac{1}{4}$ ช้อนชา กุ้งแห้ง 2 ช้อนโต๊ะ	
ซ้อสแม็กกี้ 1 ช้อนชา	
พริกแดงหั่นเป็นเส้นยาวๆ 1 เม็ด	
ผักชี 1 กิ่ง น้ำมันพืช 1 ถ้วย	

วิธีทำ

หั่นสับปะรด หอมใหญ่ หมู ขนมบัง
เป็น 4 เหลี่ยมลูกเต๋า ทอดขนมบังพอ
เหลืองอ่อนๆ พักไว้
ทอดกุ้งแห้งให้กรอบพักไว้
ใช้น้ำมันพืชที่เหลือ ผัดหมูกับหอมใหญ่
พอสุกเติมน้ำปลา ผงชูรสซ้อสแม็กกี้
แล้ว เติมข้าวผัดต่อไปจนเข้าเนื้อกันดีใส่
สับปะรดผัดต่อไปอีก 2 นาที เทใส่จาน
โรยด้วยกุ้งแห้งทอด ขนมบังทอด ตบ
แต่งด้วยพริกแดงและผักชี

หมายเหตุ ถ้าเสริฟในลูกสับปะรดจะ
สวยมาก วิธีทำสับปะรดล้างสับปะรด
ให้สะอาดตัดทางด้านหัวออกต่ำลงมาจาก
ใบสัก 1" ใช้ที่ชักไส้สับปะรด กดตรง
กลางแล้วหมุนและดึงเนื้อสับประรดออก
ถ้าไม่มีที่ชักไส้ ก็ใช้มีดตัดก้านท้ายสับ-
ปะรดออกด้วยแล้ว คว้านเนื้อออกเป็น
โพรงเย็บท้ายติดกลับไปใหม่ด้วยเข็ม
หมุดรองก้นด้วยชามขนาดเดียวกัน เท
ข้าวผัดใส่ตบแต่ง

PINEAPPLE FRIED RICE

INGREDIENTS:

3 cups cooked rice
$\frac{1}{2}$ cup diced pineapple
$\frac{1}{2}$ cup pork (diced)
2 tablespoons dried shrimp
$\frac{1}{2}$ cup diced bread
2 tablespoons diced onion
$\frac{1}{4}$ teaspoon monosodium glutamate MSG.
1 teaspoon Maggie sauce
1 cup vegetable oil
1 red pepper (sliced)
1 sprig coriander

METHOD:

Dice the pork meat into approximately 3/4 inch cubes. Dice the
pineapple, onion, and bread smaller
than the pork.

Heat the oil in a frying pan. Brown
the diced bread until golden brown.
Set aside. Using the left over oil,
fry the dried shrimp until light brown.
Set aside. In the same pan use
the remaining oil to fry pork with
onion. Stir fry for 3 minutes, add
nampla, Maggie sauce and MSG,
turning over 3-4 times. Add the
rice, continue turning for 3 minutes;
add pineapple. Stir—fry for 2
minutes more. Adjust seasoning.
Spoon onto serving plate. Garnish
with fried shrimp, fried bread, red
pepper, and top with coriander
sprig. Serve hot.

Four Colors Fried rice

ข้าวสวย

ส่วน

ข้าว	4 ถ้วย
น้ำ	6 ถ้วย

วิธีทำ

    ซาวข้าวให้สะอาดเติมน้ำตามจำนวน คือข้าวสี่ถ้วยต่อน้ำหกถ้วย บีดฝาหม้อ ตั้งไฟพอเดือด ช้อนฟองทิ้ง ลดไฟลง ให้อ่อน บีดฝาให้สนิท ตั้งทิ้งไว้อีกประ- มาณ 20 นาที จนน้ำแห้ง ยกลง

BOILED RICE

INGREDIENTS:

    4 cups rice   6 cups water

METHOD:

Fill half a large pot with rice. Pour in the measured amount of water. Bring to boil. Remove all scum and boil the rice for 10 more minutes. Cover tightly and continue cooking over a very low heat until all the water has been absorbed (about 20 minutes). Well cooked rice will look dry, fluffy and will feel soft when it is pressed flat.

ข้าวผัดสีสี

1. ข้าวผัดกะปิ (สีม่วง)

ส่วน

ข้าวสุก	2 ถ้วย
กะปิ	1 ช้อนโต๊ะ
กุ้งแห้งป่น	1 ช้อนโต๊ะ
กระเทียมสับ	1 ช้อนชา
น้ำมันพืช	2 ช้อนโต๊ะ

ไข่เจียวให้บางแล้วหั่นฝอย

(ดูวิธีทำหน้า 17)

หมูหวาน	¼ ถ้วย

(ดูวิธีทำหน้า 19)

ผักชี   พริกแดงสด   หัวหอมแดงฝาน
บางๆ 1 หัว   มะนาว 1 ชิ้น

วิธีทำ

ตักข้าวใส่ชามคลุกด้วยกะปิพักไว้ ใช้น้ำ
มันทั้งหมดเจียวกระเทียมให้หอมใส่ ข้าว
ที่คลุกด้วยกะปิผัดต่อไปประมาณ 3 นาที
เทใส่ชามก้นลึกกดให้แน่นคว่ำลงในจาน
แบนโรยด้วยไข่ฝอย กุ้งแห้งป่น หอม
แดง ผักชีและพริกแดงฝานบางๆวางบน
สุดยอด วางหมูหวานลงข้างๆกับมะนาว
เสริฟ

SHRIMP PASTE FRIED RICE

(PURPLE)

INGREDIENTS:

2 cups cooked rice
1 tablespoon kapi (shrimp paste)
1 tablespoon powdered dried
   shrimp
1 clove garlic finely chopped
2 tablespoons vegetable oil
1 egg   (fried like an omelet)
   (see page   17)
½ cup cooked sweet pork   (see
   page 19 .)
   Garnish with coriander leaves
   chili, red onion (chopped fine)
1 piece of lime or lemon

METHOD :

Put the rice in a bowl.   Add kapi,
mix well.   Heat frying pan, add 2
tablespoons vegetable oil and cook
chopped garlic until golden brown.
Add rice and cook for 3 minutes.
Remove from heat and put into a
small deep bowl.   (Jello mold).
Press down on the rice.   Turn it
over on serving plate.   Top it with
egg omelet, pounded dried shrimp,
chopped red onion, pepper sliced
thin; place cooked sweet pork to
one side.   Serve hot. (Two servings).

2. ข้าวผัดไก่ผัดพริก (สีขาว)

ส่วน

ไก่เนื้อล้วนๆ หั่นเป็นชิ้นเล็กๆ $\frac{1}{2}$ ถ้วย

พริกชี้ฟ้า (หั่นเป็นเส้นไม่ใช้เม็ด) 3 เม็ด

ใบโหระพา (หรือดอกบร๊อคคอลี่ $\frac{1}{2}$ ถ้วย)

	10	ใบ
กระเทียมสับ	1	ช้อนชา
น้ำปลา	1	ช้อนโต๊ะ
ข้าวสุก	2	ถ้วย
น้ำมันพืช	3	ช้อนโต๊ะ

วิธีทำ

เจียวกระเทียมจนเหลืองอ่อน ๆ ใส่เนื้อ
ไก่ผัดต่อไปสัก 2 นาทีเติมน้ำปลา พริก
(ดอกบร๊อคคอลี่) ผัดต่อไปอีก 3 นาที
ใส่ใบโหระพายกลงรับประทานร้อน ๆ

หมายเหตุ ถ้าไม่มีโหระพา ใช้ดอก
บร๊อคคอลี่ฝานบางๆ แทน

3. ข้าวผัดมันกุ้ง (สีส้ม)

ส่วน

กุ้งปอกล้างชักเส้นดำหั่นเป็นชิ้น $\frac{1}{2}$ ถ้วย

มันกุ้ง	1	ช้อนโต๊ะ
กระเทียมสับ	1	ช้อนชา
น้ำปลา	1	ช้อนโต๊ะ
น้ำมันพืช	2	ช้อนโต๊ะ
หอมสับเป็นชิ้นเล็กๆ	1	ช้อนโต๊ะ
ข้าวสุก	2	ถ้วย

132

CHICKEN FRIED RICE WITH CHILI PEPPER

(WHITE)

INGREDIENTS :

$\frac{1}{2}$ cup chicken breasts sliced thin

3 chili peppers (remove seeds and cut in small pieces)

10 leaves sweet basil or

$\frac{1}{2}$ cup sliced thin broccoli

1 teaspoon chopped garlic

2 tablespoons nampla(fish sauce)

2 cups cooked rice

3 tablespoons vegetable oil

METHOD :

Heat frying pan add the vegetable oil. Brown chopped garlic. Add chicken and cook for 2 minutes. Add nampla, chili, rice. Cook for 3 more minutes ; add sweet basil or broccoli and toss lightly. Serve hot.

SHRIMP FRIED RICE

(ORANGE)

INGREDIENTS:

$\frac{1}{2}$ cup shrimp shelled and cleaned (medium size)

1 tablespoon of shrimp fat

1 teaspoon chopped garlic

1 tablespoon nampla (fish sauce)

2 tablespoons vegetable oil

1 tablespoon minced white onion

2 cups cooked rice

cucumbers, spring onion, coriander leaves(Garnish)

วิธีทำ

เจียวกระเทียมพอหอมใส่กุ้งผัดสัก 1 นาที
ใส่มันกุ้ง หอมสับ น้ำปลาผัดต่อไปจน
เข้าเนื้อกันดี ใส่ข้าว ผัดต่อไปอีก 3 นาที
ตักใส่จานรับประทานร้อนๆ
หมายเหตุ มันกุ้งของพันท้ายนรสิงห์ มี
ขายเป็นขวด

METHOD :

Heat frying pan and add oil. Brown
chopped garlic. Add shrimp, shrimp
fat, chopped onion, nampla; cook
for two minutes. Add rice ; cook
for 3 more minutes. Remove from
heat and pour "Fried Rice" on a
serving plate. Sprinkle with coriander. Garnish with cucumber and
spring onions. Makes 2 servings.

4. ข้าวผัดกะหรี่ (สีเหลือง)

ส่วน

เนื้อไก่หั่นเป็นชิ้นเล็กๆ	$\frac{1}{2}$ ถ้วย
หัวหอมหั่นเป็นชิ้นเล็กๆ	1 ช้อนโต๊ะ
ลูกเกด	1 ช้อนโต๊ะ
ผงกะหรี่	1 ช้อนชา
เกลือ	1 ช้อนชา
ข้าวสุก	2 ถ้วย
น้ำมันพืช	3 ช้อนโต๊ะ

มะนาว, มะเขือเทศ อย่างละ 1 ผล

วิธีทำ

เทน้ำมันใส่กะทะ ทอดหอมให้เป็นสี
เหลืองอ่อนๆ ใส่ไก่ เกลือผงกะหรี่ ผัด
จนทุกอย่างเข้าเนื้อกันดี ใส่ข้าว ผัดต่อ
ไปอีก 3 นาทีใส่ลูกเกด เทใส่จาน ตบ
แต่งด้วยมะนาวและมะเขือเทศ

CHICKEN FRIED RICE

(YELLOW)

INGREDIENTS :

$\frac{1}{2}$ cup chicken breast sliced thin
1 tablespoon chopped onion
1 tablespoon raisins
1 teaspoon salt
1 teaspoon curry powder
3 tablespoons vegetable oil
2 cups cooked rice
1 tomato and 1 piece of lemon
  or lime

METHOD :

Heat the frying pan, add chopped
onion. Fry until light brown. Add
chicken, salt, curry powder ; cook
for 2 minutes. Add rice. Cook for
2 or 3 minutes more. Add raisins.
Remove from heat to serving plate.
Decorate with tomato and lime.

Rice with chicken and Cashewnuts

The dried black mushroom is a Chinese delicacy. You may not be able to find it in a supermarket. There are many Chinese markets that you will have no trouble finding.

This chicken dish can be cooked and served together with few other dishes as a complete dinner for the family. The idea suggested here is for one dish lunch or an individual dinner.

ข้าวราดหน้าไก่ เม็ดมะม่วง หิมพานต์ และพริกแห้งทอด

ส่วน

ข้าวสุก	3	ถ้วย
เนื้ออกไก่ล้วนๆหั่น	1	ถ้วย
เห็ดหอมหั่น	3	ดอก
หอมใหญ่หั่น 4 เหลี่ยม	½	ถ้วย
เม็ดมะม่วงหิมพานต์	½	ถ้วย
พริกแห้ง	2	เม็ด
ก้านเซลเลอรี่หั่น	½	ถ้วย
ผงชูรส	½	ช้อนชา
น้ำปลา	1	ช้อนโต๊ะ
ซีอิ๊วญี่ปุ่น	1	ช้อนชา
ผงกระเทียมเกลือ	1	ช้อนชา
แป้งมันละลายน้ำ	2	ช้อนโต๊ะ
น้ำมัน น้ำซุป อย่างละ	½	ถ้วย
พริกดอง มะนาว ผักชี	มะเขือเทศ	

สำหรับตบแต่ง

วิธีทำ

ชุบพิมพ์วงแหวนในน้ำพอเปียก เทข้าว
สุกร้อน ๆ 3 ถ้วยอัดให้แน่นเทใส่จาน
สำหรับเสริฟไว้ ทอดพริกแห้งด้วยไฟ
อ่อนตักขึ้นใช้กรรไกรตัดเป็นชิ้นๆ พัก
ไว้ น้ำมันที่เหลือใช้ผัดไก่และหอมให้
เข้ากัน โรยด้วยเกลือกระเทียมผงผัดต่อ
ไปเติมน้ำปลา ซีอิ๊ว ญี่ปุ่น ก้านเซล-
เลอรี่ เห็ดหอม เติมน้ำซุปปิดฝาไว้สัก
5 นาที พอเดือดใส่แป้งมันคนให้เข้ากัน
ใส่เม็ดมะม่วงหิมพานต์ และพริกแห้งตัก
ใส่ตรงกลางของข้าว ตบแต่งรอบๆ จาน
ด้วย มะนาว ผักชี และมะเขือเทศ
เสริฟร้อน ๆ

RICE WITH CHICKEN, CASHEW NUTS AND DRIED CHILIES

INGREDIENTS:

3 cups cooked rice
1 cup sliced chicken breasts
3 dried black mushrooms
½ cup diced onion (sugar lump size)
½ cup cashew nuts
2 dried chilies
½ cup chopped celery stalk
½ teaspoon MSG.
1 tablespoon nampla
1 tablespoon soy sauce
1 teaspoon garlic salt
1 tablespoon cornstarch mixed with 1 tablespoon water
½ cup chicken broth
½ cup vegetable oil
½ cup pickled chili (page 2)
Some lemon, coriander and tomato to garnish.

METHOD:

Press the cooked rice into a wet ring mold. Remove to serving plate. Heat the oil in the frying pan. Fry the dried chilies, cut with scissors, set aside. Using the left over oil, fry the chicken and onion; sprinkle with garlic salt and MSG, keep turning until light brown. Add chopped celery, black mushroom, nampla, soy sauce and chicken broth. Cover, simmer for 5 minutes. Add the cornstarch, stir until thickens, add cashew nuts and turn over lightly. Spoon into the center of the rice ring, top with dried chili, and garnish with lemon, tomato, and coriander leaves. Serve.

Chili beef

I have found that many of my American friends who lived in Bangkok preferred this dish to most other dishes for lunch. We stopped at the Majestic Hotel on Rajdamnern Avenue often on our way back from the Sunday market or from Pahurad. We also took it as supper at the Don Mueng Airport restaurant on the many occasions we saw our friends departing Bangkok. This dish should bring warm memories to Mariam Persons, Terry Mullinix and my former colleagues at International School of Bangkok.

ข้าวราดหน้าเนื้อพริก

ส่วน

ข้าวสุก	3	ถ้วย
เนื้อหั่น	1	ถ้วย
ข้าวโพดอ่อน	½	ถ้วย
พริกหวานหั่น	½	ถ้วย
เห็ด	½	ถ้วย
พริกเผ็ดหั่น	1	ช้อนโต๊ะ
หอมใหญ่หั่น	1	หัว
น้ำปลา	1	ช้อนโต๊ะ
ซีอิ๊วญี่ปุ่น	1	ช้อนโต๊ะ
น้ำมันหอย	2	ช้อนโต๊ะ
แป้งสาลี	1	ช้อนโต๊ะ
น้ำตาลสีรำ	1	ช้อนโต๊ะ
ขิง	1	แว่น
ผงกระเทียม	½	ช้อนชา
ผงชูรส นิดหน่อย		
น้ำ	½	ถ้วย
น้ำมัน	½	ถ้วย

วิธีทำ

หั่นผักต่างๆ แยกไว้เป็นกองๆ หั่นเนื้อ
เป็นชิ้นยาว ๆ บางๆ ใส่ชามแล้วตำขิง
ให้ละเอียดใส่ลงในเนื้อพร้อมทั้งน้ำตาล
สีรำ ผงชูรส ซีอิ๊วญี่ปุ่นและผงกระเทียม
เคล้าให้เข้ากันดี โรยแป้งสาลีหมักทิ้งไว้
1 ชม. ตักข้าวสุกใส่พิมพ์กลมกดให้แน่น
เทใส่จานเสริฟตั้งกะทะไฟแรง ๆ ใส่น้ำ
มันผัดเนื้อใส่ผักทุกอย่างผัด ต่อไปใส่
น้ำปลา น้ำมันหอยและน้ำปิดฝาไว้สัก
3 นาที ตักราดบนข้าว เสริฟร้อนๆ
สำหรับ 2 คน

CHILI BEEF

INGREDIENTS:

3 cups cooked rice
1 cup sliced beef (round steak)
½ cup young baby corn
½ cup chopped bell pepper
1 tablespoon chopped hot
  pepper
½ cup mushrooms
1 medium onion (sliced)
1 tablespoon nampla (fish sauce)
1 tablespoon soy sauce
2 tablespoons oyster sauce
1 tablespoon flour
1 tablespoon brown sugar
1 slice ginger (pounded)
½ teaspoon garlic powder
  dash monosodium glutamate
  (MSG.)
½ cup water or beef broth
½ cup vegetable oil

METHOD:

Chop all the vegetables, wash and
drain.

Slice beef with a sharp knife into
paper-thin slices 2 inches by 1
inch. Combine meat, pounded
ginger, brown sugar, MSG, soy sauce
garlic powder and flour. Marinate
for 1 hour.

Press the rice into a wet mold.
Remove to serving plate.

Heat the oil in wok or saucepan over
medium high heat and brown the
beef for 2 minutes. Add the chopped
vegetables, stir-fry for 2 minutes,
add the water or beef broth. Cover,
and simmer for 3 minutes. Add
nampla and oyster sauce, tossing
lightly, and spoon over the rice.
Makes 2 servings.

Shrimp and chicken Chop-Suey

Chopsuey is so well indentified with a Chinese menu that even in this Thai cookbook I decide to borrow the name for the dish with bean sprouts and Chinese green. The dish has a mild taste, also characteristic of Chinese dish. You should combine this dish with other sharp tasted dishes for a balanced dinner menu.

ช๊อบสุ่ยไก่กุ้ง

CHICKEN AND SHRIMP CHOP SUEY

ส่วน

กุ้งปอกล้างผ่าหลัง	½ ถ้วย
ไก่เนื้อล้วนๆ หั่น	½ ถ้วย
ก้านเซเลอรี่หั่น	2 ช้อนโต๊ะ
หน่อไม้หั่น	2 ช้อนโต๊ะ
เห็ดผ่าครึ่ง	2 ช้อนโต๊ะ
ผักกาดเขียวหั่น (กวางตุ้ง)	½ ถ้วย
ถั่วงอกตัดหัวตัดท้าย	½ ถ้วย
น้ำปลา	1 ช้อนโต๊ะ
ซีอิ๊วใส	1 ช้อนโต๊ะ
น้ำมันหอย	2 ช้อนโต๊ะ
ผงชูรส	½ ช้อนชา
แบ๋งมันละลายน้ำ	2 ช้อนโต๊ะ
น้ำ	½ ถ้วย
ผงกระเทียม	½ ช้อนชา
น้ำมัน	½ ถ้วย

วิธีทำ หั่นผักต่าง ๆ แช่น้ำไว้สัก 10 นาที เอาขึ้นแยกไว้เป็นกองๆ หั่นไก่ กุ้ง ใส่จานช่องไว้ ตั้งกะทะน้ำมัน ไฟแรงๆ ผัดไก่ กุ้ง โรยด้วยผงกระเทียมเติมน้ำปลา ซีอิ๊วใส น้ำมันหอย ผงชูรส ผัดพอไก่ กุ้ง สุก ใส่ผักต่าง ๆเติมน้ำปิดฝาทิ้งไว้ 5 นาที เปิดฝาเติมแบ๋งมันคนให้ทั่ว พอแบ๋งสุก เทใส่จานเสิร์ฟร้อนกับข้าว 3-4 คน

CHICKEN AND SHRIMP CHOP SUEY

INGREDIENTS:

½ cup medium shrimp

½ cup sliced chicken breast (raw)

2 tablespoons chopped celery stalk

2 tablespoons chopped bamboo shoots

2 tablespoons mushrooms cut in halves

½ cup Chinese green (Buk Choy)

½ cup bean sprouts

1 tablespoon soy sauce

1 tablespoon oyster sauce

½ teaspoon Monosodium Glutamate (MSG.)

1 tablespoon corn starch mixed with 1 tablespoon water

½ cup water

½ teaspoon garlic powder

½ cup vegetable oil

METHOD:

Chop all the vegetables, soak in water for 10 minutes and drain. Slice the chicken; clean and cut the shrimp.

Heat the oil in a saucepan over medium heat; fry the chicken and shrimp; sprinkle with garlic and MSG; add soy sauce, nampla, and oyster sauce, stirring until the meat is cooked. Add the vegetables, turn for a few times, then add water. Cover and simmer for 5 minutes. Slowly add cornstarch and stir until thickened. Spoon onto a serving plate; serve with rice.

Fried shrimp and broccoli

There is a method to keep broccoli crispy in your dish. You must soak them in water for at least 15 minutes before frying. Many of the fine Thai or Chinese restaurants do not have this knowledge which is shameful.

You may substitute beef or chicken for the shrimp.

บร๊อคคอลี่ผัดกุ้ง

ส่วน

กุ้งตัวใหญ่	5	ตัว
บรอคคอลี่หั่นเป็นแว่นๆ	2	ถ้วย
กระเทียมทุบ	1	ช้อนชา
น้ำปลา	1	ช้อนโต๊ะ
น้ำมันหอย	1	ช้อนโต๊ะ
น้ำมัน	2	ช้อนโต๊ะ

วิธีทำ

ปอกกุ้งล้างชักเส้นดำหั่น หั่นบร๊อคคอลี่
เป็นแว่นๆ แช่น้ำทิ้งไว้ 15 นาที   ตั้ง
กะทะไฟร้อนปานกลาง เจียวกระเทียม
พอเหลือง ใส่กุ้งผัดพอกุ้งสุกใส่น้ำปลา
ผัก (หยิบขึ้นจากน้ำแล้วใส่กะทะเลย)
ผัดต่อไปสัก 3 นาทีเติมน้ำมันหอยคนให้
ทั่วผักและกุ้งตักใส่จานเสริฟร้อนๆ รับ-
ประทานกับข้าว

FRIED BROCCOLI WITH SHRIMP

INGREDIENTS:

5 large shrimp
2 cups sliced broccoli
1 teaspoon minced garlic
1 teaspoon nampla (fish sauce)
1 tablespoon oyster sauce
2 tablespoons vegetable oil

METHOD:

Peel the shrimp, remove the center
back line, cut and clean. Soak
sliced broccoli in cold water for 15
minutes.

Heat the oil in frying pan over
medium heat. Fry the minced
garlic until golden brown. Add the
shrimp, turning over a few times.
Add nampla and oyster sauce and
stir—fry. Drain the broccoli, add to
the fried shrimp, and stir for 3 minutes. Spoon onto a serving plate.
Serve with rice.

Asparagus with Lobster sauce

This dish is not really Thai since I do not substitute asparagus for any Thai vegetable. I first found this dish at Chuladul Thai Restaurant in Culver City, California. The dish as described here does not differ much from what is served there.

If you use canned asparagus, please heat asparagus until warm before arranging on serving plate.

แอสปารากัสราดล๊อบสเตอร์ซ๊อส

ส่วน

แอสปารากัสสดหรือกระป๋อง	1 ปอนด์
	(½ กิโล)
น้ำตาล	1 ช้อนชา
หมูบด 1 ถ้วยผสมกับน้ำเย็น	2 ช้อนโต๊ะ
เนื้อปูแกะแล้ว	½ ถ้วย
ไข่ตีเบาๆ	1 ฟอง
หอมใหญ่สับ	1 ช้อนโต๊ะ
ต้นหอมหั่นละเอียด	1 ช้อนชา
น้ำปลา	1 ช้อนโต๊ะ
น้ำมันหอย	1 ช้อนโต๊ะ
พริกไทย	¼ ช้อนชา
แป้งมันละลายน้ำ	1 ช้อนโต๊ะ
น้ำมันพืช	2 ช้อนโต๊ะ

วิธีทำ

ตัดก้านแข็ง ๆ ของต้นแอสปารากัสออก ทิ้งใช้แต่ส่วนอ่อนๆ ต้มในน้ำ เดือด 3 นาทีใส่น้ำตาลลงไปแล้ว ตักขึ้นผึ่งให้ สะเด็ดน้ำจัดใส่จานเสริฟ ตั้งกะทะไฟ ร้อนปานกลาง ใส่น้ำมันทอดหอมสับพอ เหลืองใส่หมูบดและเนื้อปู น้ำปลา น้ำ มันหอย ผัดให้เข้ากันใส่แป้ง หมั่นคน อย่าให้แป้งเบ็นลูก พอแป้งสุกใส่พริก ไทยและไข่คนต่อไปพอไข่สุกใส่ต้นหอม แล้วเทราดลงบนแอสปารากัสต้ม เสริฟ ร้อนๆ กับข้าว

ASPARAGUS WITH LOBSTER SAUCE

INGREDIENTS:

1 pound fresh or canned Asparagus
1 teaspoon sugar
1 cup ground pork; add 2 tablespoons water
½ cup crab meat
1 egg slightly beaten
1 tablespoon minced onion
1 tablespoon nampla
1 tablespoon oyster sauce
¼ teaspoon pepper
1 tablespoon cornstarch mixed with 1 tablespoon water
2 tablespoons vegetable oil

METHOD:

Clean the asparagus and remove tough end. Cook uncovered in boiling water for 3 minutes Add sugar and drain. Arrange on serving plate.

Heat the oil in the saucepan over medium heat. Brown the onion until light brown. Stir in ground pork and crab meat. Add nampla and oyster sauce. Stir-fry for 3 minutes, add the cornstarch, lower the heat, and stir until the sauce is thickened. Pour in the beaten egg very slowly, when slightly set; give the sauce a stir. Pour the mixture over the cooked asparagus. Serve with rice. Makes 2 serving.

Abalone in Oyster sauce

Professer Peter K. Stein of the famous Measurement Engineering Lab at Arizona State always tells his students that when you cross a crocodile with abalone you will get "croco balone". We showed him that the abalone that he talked about was delicious. The Chinese also consider abalone one of the best dishes on their table.

หอยโข่งทะเล (เป๋าฮื้อ) น้ำแดง

ส่วน

หอยโข่งทะเล	1	กระป๋อง
ผักกาดหอมใบอ่อนๆ	10	ใบ
เห็ดหอม	5	ดอก
กระเทียมสับ	1	ช้อนชา
ซีอิ๊วใส	1	ช้อนโต๊ะ
น้ำมันหอย	2	ช้อนโต๊ะ
แป้งมันละลายน้ำ	3	ช้อนโต๊ะ
ต้นหอมหั่น	½	ถ้วย
น้ำมัน	½	ถ้วย

วิธีทำ

หั่นหอยโข่งทะเลเป็นชิ้นบางๆ เก็บน้ำ
ไว้, แช่เห็ดหอมในน้ำอุ่นไว้สัก 10 นาที
หั่นต้นหอมเป็นท่อนๆ แล้วล้างรวมไว้
กับผักกาดหอม
ตั้งกะทะเจียวกระเทียมให้เหลืองใส่หอย
โข่งทะเลและเห็ดหอมผัดกลับไปกลับมา
จนทั่ว ใส่ซีอิ๊วใส น้ำมันหอย และน้ำ
จากกระป๋องครึ่งหนึ่ง พอน้ำเดือดใส่
แป้งคนจนแป้งสุกใส่ผักกาดหอมและต้น
หอมผัดต่อไปเพียง 1 นาที ยกลงตักใส่
จานเสริฟร้อนๆ กับข้าว

ABALONE WITH OYSTER SAUCE

INGREDIENTS :
- 1 can abalone
- 10 leaves Romain lettuce
- 5 dried black mushrooms (see glossary)
- 1 teaspoon minced garlic
- 1 tablespoon soy sauce
- 2 tablespoons oyster sauce
- 2 tablespoons cornstarch mixed with 1 tablespoon water
- ½ cup spring onion cut into 2 inch segments including top
- ½ cup vegetable oil

METHOD :

Slice the abalone with a sharp knife in paper thin slices (save the juice). Soak the black mushooms in warm water for 10 minutes. Remove the stump. Cut the spring onion and Romain lettuce; soak in water and drain. Heat the oil in a large saucepan on medium heat. Fry the minced garlic until golden brown. Add abalone and black mushrooms. Turn over a few times. Add soy sauce, oyster sauce and half a can of abalone juice. Bring it to the boil. Add cornstarch stirring until the gravy is thickened. Add lettuce and spring onions, turning over a few times. Remove from heat. Spoon onto a serving plate and serve hot with rice.

Roast red pork

I have to admit again that a roast pork is not a Thai dish. It is known all over the world as Chinese dish, and the best that I have found was in Hong Kong. I must confess that I have never been to the Chinese Mainland or England, so I can not be very sure.

Roast pork is very popular in Thailand and I found this method of preparing it quite easy. I do hope you will agree.

หมูแดง

ส่วน

หมูสันใน 2 ปอนด์	(1 กิโล)
ขิงต่ำละเอียด	1 ช้อนชา
ผงอบเชย	½ ช้อนชา
ซีอิ้ว	2 ช้อนโต๊ะ
แม่โขงวิสกี้	1 ช้อนโต๊ะ
ซ้อสฮอยซิน	2 ช้อนโต๊ะ
สีแดง	½ ช้อนชา
แป้งสาลีละลายน้ำ	1 ช้อนโต๊ะ
น้ำสุก	½ ถ้วย
น้ำปลา	1 ช้อนชา
น้ำมันพืช	1 ช้อนโต๊ะ

วิธีทำ

หยอดสีแดงลงบนเนื้อหมูเคล้าด้วยมือให้สีแดงทั่วกันใส่ขิงสับ อบเชย และซีอิ้ว ซ้อสฮอยซินและวิสกี้ เคล้าให้เข้ากันดี เติมน้ำมันพืชและหมักทิ้งไว้ 2 ชั่วโมง เปิดเตาอบไฟ 375° ปูกระดาษตะกั่วบนถาดสำหรับอบวางหมูแดงตามยาวเข้าอบประมาณ 30 นาที หั่นเป็นชิ้นบางๆ จัดใส่จานไว้น้ำมันที่เหลือในถาด เทใส่กะทะผสมด้วยน้ำสุก น้ำปลาตั้งไฟพอเดือด ละลายแป้งสาลีลงไป คนอย่าให้เป็นลูกใช้เป็นน้ำซ้อสราดลงบนหมูที่หั่นใส่จานไว้แล้ว, เสริฟ

ROASTED RED PORK

INGREDIENTS:

2 pounds (1 kilo) lean pork
1 teaspoon minced ginger
½ teaspoon cinnamon
2 tablespoons soy sauce
1 tablespoon whisky
2 tablespoons Hoi–Sin sauce
(see glossary)
½ teaspoon red food coloring
1 tablespoon flour mixed with
1 tablespoon water
1 teaspoon nampla (fish sauce)
1 tablespoon vegetable oil

METHOD:

Cut the pork into large chunks (like stewing beef) and put in a bowl. Drop the food coloring on the pork and rub until the meat turns red. Add minced ginger, cinnamon, Hoi Sin sauce, soy sauce and whisky; mix well. Add the vegetable oil. Marinate for 2 hours.
Pre–heat the oven to 375°. Place the pork in a roasting pan or pyrex dish, in a single layer. Pour the marinade sauce over and roast for 30 minutes. Remove the roast pork, cool, slice and arrange on a serving plate. Use the drippings in the pan to make gravy by adding ½ cup hot water, stir well and bring to boil. Add nampla and the flour mixed with water; stir until the gravy thickens. Pour over the pork slices and serve.

Bar-be-cue sliced beef

This dish is somewhat like "Mongolian Bar-be-cue" which is famous in many Chinese Restaurants. Our preparation is a little different to cater to Thai taste. You will find it quite acceptable, I am sure.

เนื้อย่างโอชา

ส่วน

เนื้อสะโพกแล่บาง 2×2"   2 ปอนด์
                         (1 กิโล)

ซีอิ๊วญี่ปุ่น   3 ช้อนโต๊ะ

น้ำขิงสด   1 ช้อนโต๊ะ

น้ำตาลสีร่ำ   1 ช้อนโต๊ะ

ต้นหอมหั่นละเอียด   1 ช้อนโต๊ะ

น้ำมันพืช   1 ช้อนโต๊ะ

แม่โขง วิสกี้   1 ช้อนโต๊ะ

ผักสำหรับแต่งรอบจาน   ผักกาดหอม

ต้นหอม มะเขือเทศ สับปะรด

วิธีทำ

เนื้อที่แล่บางๆ ใส่ลงในชามก้นลึก ราด
ด้วยน้ำขิงเคล้าให้ทั่วเนื้อเติมน้ำตาลสีร่ำ
ซีอิ๊วญี่ปุ่น น้ำมันและต้นหอมหั่น หมัก
ทิ้งไว้อย่างน้อย 2 ชั่วโมง   พร้อมด้วย
แม่โขง

ตบแต่งจานเปลด้วยผักทั้งสามอย่าง พอ
จะรับประทาน   ย่างเนื้อบนไฟแรง ๆ
ข้างละ 1 นาที จัดใส่จานเปลเสริฟร้อนๆ

BAR-BE-CUE SLICED BEEF

INGREDIENTS:

   2 pounds (1 kilo) roast beef
      meat, sliced thin.
   3 tablespoons soy sauce (Kicko-
      man)
   1 tablespoon ginger root juice
   1 tablespoon light brown sugar
   1 tablespoon chopped spring
      onion
   1 tablesoon vegetable oil
   1 tablespoon whisky (optional)
      Garnish with lettuce, spring
      onions, tomatoes pineapple,
      etc. as desired.

METHOD:

In a large bowl combine the thinly
sliced beef, ginger juice, light brown
sugar, soy sauce, whisky and oil.
Sprinkle with spring onions. Marinate
for 2 hours.   Arrange a serving
plate with the vegetable garnishes.
Charcoal broil the meat 1 minute on
each side (or until the pink is gone).
Place on serving plate. Serve warm.

NOTE:

To extract juice from ginger root,
Pound in mortar, add a small
amount of water and squeeze.

Bean cake Soup

Bean cake can be found in two inches by two inches square and one inch thick in Chinese markets. It can also be found in a sausage like roll in Japanese markets. You may well find them in the super markets also. This soup is good for breakfast, lunch, dinner or supper. It is quite nourishing and very easy to digest.

There is a trick here which even some restaurants do not know. You must put ground pork mixture in cold water and heat the whole content. Do not put the pork mixture into hot water. It will not look and taste as good.

แกงจืดเต้าหู้

ส่วน

เต้าหู้หลอด (หั่นหนาชิ้นละ $\frac{1}{2}$")

	1 หลอด
หมูบด	$\frac{1}{2}$ ถ้วย
กระเทียมผง	$\frac{1}{2}$ ช้อนชา
เกลือ	$\frac{1}{2}$ ช้อนชา
น้ำปลา	1 ช้อนโต๊ะ
น้ำ	3 ถ้วย

ต้นหอมตัดเป็นท่อนๆละ 1" 2 ต้น

พริกไทยนิดหน่อย

ผงชูรส $\frac{1}{2}$ ช้อนโต๊ะ

วิธีทำ

เคล้าหมูบดกับกระเทียมผง และน้ำปลา $\frac{1}{2}$ ช้อนโต๊ะ ขยำหมูที่ผสมแล้วในน้ำเย็น ตั้งไฟจนน้ำเดือดเติมน้ำปลา เกลือ ผง ชูรสและเต้าหู้ พอน้ำเดือดใส่ต้นหอม แล้วตักใส่ชามโรยด้วยผักชี และพริก ไทย เสริฟร้อน ๆ

BEAN CAKE SOUP

INGREDIENTS :
1 bar bean cake cut into pieces
$\frac{1}{2}$ cup ground pork
$\frac{1}{2}$ teaspoon garlic powder
$\frac{1}{2}$ teaspoon salt
1 tablespoon nampla (fish sauce)
3 cups water
2 spring onions cut into 1 inch
    segments
1 sprig coriander
Dash pepper
$\frac{1}{2}$ teaspoon monosodium gluta-
    mate (MSG)

METHOD :
Combine ground pork, garlic powder, salt and MSG. Mix well. In a soup pot, put cold water and the ground pork mixture, stir. Bring slowly to the boil. Add bean cake, nam pla and simmer for 3 minutes. Add spring onions. Spoon into a serving dish. Dash with pepper and top with coriander. Serve.

Sweet and Sour Chicken Wings

ผัดเปรี้ยวหวานปีกไก่

ส่วน

ปีกไก่ใช้เฉพาะโคนปีก	10	ปีก
แป้งสาลี	2	ช้อนโต๊ะ
แป้งข้าวโพด	2	ช้อนโต๊ะ
เกลือ	½	ช้อนชา
น้ำเย็น	2	ช้อนโต๊ะ
นมสด	1	ช้อนโต๊ะ
น้ำมันพืช	1	ช้อนโต๊ะ
น้ำมันพืชสำหรับทอด	2	ถ้วย

หัวหอมหั่นเป็นชิ้นใหญ่ (1 หัวหั่นเป็น 8 ชิ้น) 1 หัว

SWEET AND SOUR CHICKEN WINGS

INGREDIENTS:

- 10 chicken wings
- 2 tablespoons flour
- 2 tablespoons cornstarch
- ½ teaspoon salt
- 2 tablespoons water
- 1 tablespoon light cream
- 1 tablespoon vegetable oil
- 2 cups vegetable oil to deep fry
- 1 large onion cut into eight pieces

พริกระฆัง(หั่นชิ้นใหญ่ๆ) 1 เม็ด
มะเขือเทศ (หั่นชิ้นใหญ่) 2 ผล
สับปะรดหั่น ½ ถ้วย
น้ำตาลทราย 2 ช้อนโต๊ะ
น้ำส้ม 1 ช้อนโต๊ะ
เกลือ 1 ช้อนชา
น้ำ 2 ช้อนโต๊ะ
แป้งมันผสมน้ำ 2 ช้อนโต๊ะ
ซ้อสมะเขือเทศ 1 ช้อนโต๊ะ

วิธีทำ

น้ำซ้อส ใช้หม้อเคลือบใบเล็ก ผสมน้ำ
ตาลทราย เกลือ น้ำส้ม ซ๊อส มะเขือเทศ
น้ำ ตั้งไฟให้เดือด ค่อยเทแป้งมันคนให้
เข้ากันดียกลงพักไว้ (หรือจะทำจำนวน
มาก ใส่ขวดเก็บในตู้เย็นก็ได้)

แป้ง ผสมแป้งข้าวโพด แป้งสาลี
เกลือ ร่อนเข้าด้วยกันเทนม น้ำ น้ำมัน
ตีจนเข้ากันดี พักไว้

ไก่ใช้เฉพาะโคนปีก รูดเนื้อไก่ให้มาอยู่
ปลายปีกส่วนใหญ่ทางเดียวชุบลงในส่วน
ผสมแป้ง ทอดในน้ำมันร้อนจัดจน
เหลืองจัดใส่จาน ใช้น้ำมันเล็กน้อยผัด
หัวหอม พริกระฆัง พอสุกเติมด้วย
ซ้อสที่ผสมไว้แล้วผัดให้เข้ากันดี เติม
สับปะรดและมะเขือเทศ เทราดบนปีก
ไก่ทอดเสริฟทันที

1 bell pepper cut into eight
  pieces
2 medium tomatoes cut into
  eight pieces
½ cup cut pineapple
2 tablespoons sugar
1 tablespoon vinegar
1 teaspoon salt
2 tablespoons cornstarch
  mixed with 1 tablespoon water
2 tablespoons water
1 tablespoon tomato paste

METHOD:

Blend the flour, cornstarch, salt, 2
tablespoons water, light cream and
1 tablespoon vegetable oil into a
runny batter; beat with fork or
rotary beater and set aside.

In a small saucepan combine sugar,
vinegar, salt and 2 tablespoons
water. Boil together until syrupy;
add tomato paste and stir well.
Add cornstarch, moistened with
water, stirring until the sauce thickens. Set aside.

Cut and bone the chicken wings.
Move the meat to one end of the
bone. Coat the chicken wings sticks
in batter and deep fry until golden
brown. Drain and arrange on a
serving plate. In a large frying pan,
heat 2 tablespoons oil on medium
heat; stir—fry the cut onion and
bell pepper for 2 minutes. Add the
sauce and gently turn. Add tomato
and pineapple. Toss lightly, pour
over the fried chicken wings, and
serve.

Shrimp with butter sauce

      In Bangkok, fresh water shrimp can still be found in the market places. I do not know whether it would be as easy in the US supermarkets. Frozen shrimp can be used, they are clean, just set it to thaw out before you rub them with garlic salt and butter.

กุ้งอบเนย

ส่วน

กุ้งใหญ่ตัวงามๆ	6 ตัว
ผงกระเทียมเกลือ	½ ช้อนชา
เนยสด	3 ช้อนโต๊ะ
น้ำมะนาวคั้น	1 ช้อนชา
ผักสำหรับตบแต่ง เช่นมะเขือเทศ ต้น	
หอม มะนาวฝานเป็นชิ้นๆ	

วิธีทำ

กุ้งใหญ่ ผ่าหลังชักเส้นดำ ตัด ครีบ ชักถุงดำออก ล้าง ผึ่งให้สะเด็ดน้ำ ใช้เนย ⅓ ส่วนทาบนเนื้อกุ้ง โรยด้วยผง กระเทียมเกลือ ทุกตัว อบใต้เตาไฟแรง 475° ประมาณ 3-5 นาที จัดใส่จานตบ แต่งด้วยผักสด ละลายเนยที่เหลือ ผสม ด้วยน้ำมะนาว ใส่ถ้วยวางตรงกลางจาน กุ้งเสริฟร้อนๆ

SHRIMP WITH BUTTER SAUCE

INGREDIENTS :

- 6 large shrimp
- ½ teaspoon garlic salt
- 3 tablespoons butter
- 1 teaspoon lemon juice
  garnish with tomatoes, spring onions and thinly sliced lemon,

METHOD :

Use the sharp knife to cut the back open and remove center lines of the shrimp. Clean and drain. Rub the shrimp with garlic salt and 1 tablespoon butter. Preheat the oven to 475°F. Place the shrimp under broiler and broil for 3½ minutes. Arrange on a serving plate. Garnish with tomato, spring onions and lemon slices; melt the butter, add the lemon juice, and serve with the roasted shrimp.

Stuffed peppers

พริกหยวกสอดไส้

ส่วน

หมูบด	1	ถ้วย
หอมใหญ่หั่นละเอียด	1	ช้อนโต๊ะ
ผักชีหั่นละเอียด	1	ช้อนชา
พริกไทย	½	ช้อนชา
ผงกระเทียมเกลือ	1	ช้อนชา
ไข่ไก่	1	ฟอง
พริกหยวก (คว้านไส้ออก)	6	เม็ด
ไข่ไก่ตีเบาๆ	2	ฟอง
น้ำมันพืชสำหรับทากะทะ	1	ช้อนโต๊ะ

STUFFED PEPPERS

INGREDIENTS:

- 1 cup ground pork
- 1 tablespoon minced onion
- 1 teaspoon minced coriander
- ½ teaspoon pepper
- 1 teaspoon garlic salt
- 1 egg
- 6 peppers
- 2 slightly beaten eggs
- 2 tablespoons vegetable oil
  coriander leaves to garnish.

วิธีทำ

ผสมหมูบดเข้าด้วยกันกับหอมสับผักชี –
หั่น พริกไทย ผงกระเทียมเกลือ ไข่ไก่
เคล้าให้เข้าเนื้อกันดี สอดในไส้พริก
หยวก จัดใส่รังถึงนึ่งจนสุกประมาณ
8–10 นาที
ตั้งกะทะพอร้อนไฟอ่อน ๆ ทาด้วยน้ำมัน
ใช้นิ้วจุ่มลงในไข่ไก่ที่ตีเบา ๆ ไว้แล้วโรย
กลับไปกลับมาบนกะทะจนเป็นแผ่นบาง
เหมือนตาข่าย พอสุกตักพักไว้ทำให้
หมดไข่ ใช้ตาข่าย (ทำด้วยไข่) ห่อพริก
หยวกนึ่งจัดลงใส่จาน ตบแต่งด้วยพริก
แดงและผักชี

มะเขือชุบไข่ทอด

ส่วน

มะเขือม่วงผลงาม ๆ	1	ผล
ไข่ไก่	2	ฟอง
เกลือ	½	ช้อนชา
นมสด	1	ช้อนชา
น้ำมันพืช	1	ถ้วย

ผักสำหรับตบแต่ง พริกแดงและผักชี

วิธีทำ

ตีไข่ให้ฟู ผสมด้วยเกลือและนมสด ตี
ต่อไปให้เข้ากันฝานมะเขือม่วงตามขวาง
หนาประมาณ ½ นิ้ว ชุบลงในส่วนประ–
สมไข่ ทอดในน้ำมันร้อนจัด จนเกรียม
ตักใส่จานตบแต่งด้วยพริกแดง และผักชี

METHOD:

In a small mixing bowl, combine
ground pork, onion, coriander,
pepper, garlic salt, and egg. Mix
well. Set aside.
Remove the seeds from the pepper.
Wash and drain. Stuff with the pork
mixture, lay in the steamer. Steam
for 8–10 minutes. Rub the wok
with some oil and heat over medium
low heat. Dip your fingers into the
beaten egg. Sprinkle the egg back
and forth across the wok to make
the egg nest which is about 8
inches in diameter. Make 3 nests.
Cut each in half and wrap the
steamed peppers. Arrange on a
serving plate. Garnish with coriander leaves.

FRIED EGG PLANT

INGREDIENTS:

    1 large egg plant
    2 eggs
    1 teaspoon light cream
    ½ teaspoon salt
    1 cup vegetable oil
      some coriander and red chili
      to garnish

METHOD:

Beat the egg lightly with fork. Add
salt and light cream, stirring a few
times. Slice the eggplant ½ inch
thick. Coat each slice in the egg
mixture. Deep fry in hot oil until
golden brown. Place on a serving
plate. Garnish with coriander and
red chili.

Banana balls

Thai style fried banana which is called "Indian Banana" is adapted from Indonesia. The original Indonesian Version, however, uses jack fruit meat and seed, not banana. The version we have here is not true Thai style because we cannot find the proper type of banana. It is then something that I adapted thinking of our Thai style fried banana at home. And it is good.

กล้วยทอด

ส่วน

กล้วยหอมห่าม ๆ	6 ผล
ไข่	1 ฟอง (ตีเบาๆ)
น้ำตาล	2 ช้อนโต๊ะ
แบ่งข้าวโพด	$\frac{1}{4}$ ถ้วย
แบ่งสาลี	$\frac{3}{4}$ ถ้วย
เกลือ	1 ช้อนชา
ผงฟู	1 ช้อนชา
นมสด	$\frac{1}{2}$ ถ้วย
เนยละลาย	1 ช้อนโต๊ะ
น้ำมันพืช	2 ถ้วย
น้ำผึ้ง	2 ช้อนโต๊ะ

วิธีทำ

ร่อนแบ่งทั้งสองอย่าง ให้เข้ากันกับผงฟู
และเกลือ ตีเนยและน้ำตาลจนขึ้น ใส่
ไข่และนมและผสมด้วยส่วนแบ่งจนเข้า
เนื้อกันดี ปอกกล้วยหอม แล้วตัดลูกละ
4-5 ชิ้น ชุบลงในส่วนผสมแบ่งให้ทั่ว
กล้วย ทอดในน้ำมันมากๆ ไฟร้อนจัด
ประมาณ 3 นาที ตัดใส่กระดาษซับน้ำ-
มันเสริฟร้อนๆ กับ น้ำผึ้ง.

BANANA BALLS

INGREDIENTS:

6 firm bananas
1 egg (lightly beaten)
2 tablespoons sugar
$\frac{1}{4}$ cup corn starch
$\frac{3}{4}$ cup sifted flour
$\frac{1}{2}$ teaspoon salt
1 teaspoon baking powder
$\frac{1}{2}$ cup cream (evaporated milk)
1 tablespoon melted butter
2 cups vegetable oil
2 tablespoons honey

METHOD:

Sift together flour, baking power,
salt. Cream butter, egg, and milk
together. Add to dry ingredients,
stirring only until moistened. Peel
bananas. Cut in $1\frac{1}{2}$ inch lengths.
Dip into batter, spreading batter
evenly over bananas. Fry in hot
deep fat (375°) for 3 minutes or
until golden brown. Drain on paper
towel and serve with honey.

Custard

There are two types of Thai custard described under this one heading. The Thai word for custard is "Sankhaya". Sankhaya is made with egg, sugar and coconut cream as basic ingredients. They are not really like custard but we have not yet found any word that describe it better.

สังขยา

ส่วน

น้ำกะทิ	1	ถ้วย
น้ำตาลปีก	¾	ถ้วย (สีน้ำตาล)
น้ำตาลทรายขาว	½	ถ้วย
ไข่	4	ฟอง
หัวน้ำหอมวานิลลา	1	ช้อนชา (ถ้าชอบ)

วิธีทำ

เทน้ำกะทิลงในชามขนาดกลางใส่ไข่และ
น้ำตาลทั้งสองอย่างลงไปใช้ใบตองหรือ
ใบเตย ขยำในส่วนทั้งสามเข้ากันดี หยิบ
ใบตองหรือใบเตยออก (ถ้าชอบใส่หัว
น้ำหอมวานิลลา) เทใส่ชามแก้วกลม
ขนาด 9 นิ้ว ใส่รังถึงนึ่งประมาณ 45
นาที ยกลงแต่งหน้าด้วยฝอยทอง

(ดูวิธีทำฝอยทองหน้า 172)

หมายเหตุ หรือจะนึ่งสังขยาในฟักทอง
หรือมะพร้าวอ่อนก็ได้ตามชอบ ฟักทอง
ขนาดกลาง 1 ลูกหรือมะพร้าวอ่อนขนาด
เล็ก 3 ลูก

วุ้นสังขยา

ส่วน

เหมือนกันกับสังขยา เพิ่มวุ้นผง หนึ่ง
ซองต่อน้ำหนึ่งถ้วยครึ่งเคี่ยวไฟจนละลาย
ดีแล้ว ผสมด้วยส่วนสังขยาที่ทำไว้คน
บนไฟอ่อนๆ จนสุก คนจนเข้าเนื้อกันดี
เทใส่พิมพ์หรือถ้วยแก้วขนาดเส้นผ่าศูนย์
กลาง 3 นิ้ว ทิ้งไว้จนเย็นจะได้วุ้นสังขยา
ประมาณ 12 อัน

SANKHAYA COCONUT CUSTARD

INGREDIENTS :

1 cup   thick coconut cream

¾ cup palm sugar or brown
sugar

3 small young coconuts or 1
medium pumpkin or 9" pie
plate

4 eggs

¾ cup white sugar

METHOD:

1. Trim coconuts into nice shape.
Cut the top open not too deep and
save. Pour out the water, or scoop
out all the inside of the pumpkin
leaving the meat intact.

2. Beat the eggs and combine with
palm sugar and white sugar. Stir
until the sugar dissolves. Add
coconut milk, stir well. Pour the
mixture into the young coconut or
pumpkin or on the pie plate.

3. Heat the steam pot until the
water boils. Put the coconuts on
rack of steamer. Cover and steam
for 45 minutes. For pumpkin or pie
plate, steam for 30 minutes.

JELLY CUSTARD

Use the same ingredients as coconut
custard. Cook and stir over low
heat until mixture comes to a boil
and thickens. Set aside.

Cook 1 envelope unsweetened ge-
latin with 1 cup of water. Add the
cooked coconut custard. Mix well.
Spoon into individual custard cups
or jelly mold. Chill until ready to
serve. Makes 10 to 12 servings.

Taro balls in coconut syrup

"Bua Loi" in Thai means "Floating Lotus seed". This sweet dish is called thus because the Taro balls are like Lotus seeds. This is an old Thai dessert of obscure origin. It could have come from the west (Europe, not west of the Mississippi) or a nearby country. It is based on coconut and palm sugar. It is, of course, one of the most common Thai desserts in the whole kingdom.

ขนมบัวลอยเผือก

ส่วน

เผือกต้มแล้วบด	$\frac{1}{2}$	ถ้วย
แบ่งข้าวเจ้า	1	ถ้วย
แบ่งข้าวโพด	$\frac{1}{2}$	ถ้วย
น้ำ	$1\frac{1}{2}$	ถ้วย
น้ำกะทิ	2	ถ้วย
น้ำตาลอ้อย	2	ช้อนโต๊ะ
น้ำตาลทรายขาว	$\frac{1}{2}$	ถ้วย
เกลือ	$\frac{1}{4}$	ช้อนชา

แบ่งมันเล็กน้อยใช้ตอนปั้น

วิธีทำ

ละลายแบ่งข้าวเจ้า และแบ่งข้าวโพดกับ
น้ำ ใช้มือบี้ให้ละลายอย่าให้มีเม็ด ตั้ง
ไฟกลางๆ คนเสมอจนแบ่งสุก ตักใส่
จาน ใช้ช้อนบี้ทีละน้อยจนไม่มีเม็ด
(ทำขณะยังร้อนอยู่) แล้วนวดต่อด้วยมือ
ชุบน้ำจนเหนียวดีแล้วผสมด้วยเผือกบด
นวดต่อไปจนเข้าเนื้อกันดีใช้มือแตะแบ่ง
มันปั้นเป็นเม็ดเล็กๆ (เส้นผ่าศูนย์กลาง
$\frac{1}{2}$ นิ้ว) เรียงใส่จานไว้
ตั้งกะทิ ผสมน้ำตาลทั้งสองอย่างและ
เกลือหมั่นคนอย่าให้กะทิแตกมัน พอ
เดือดใส่แบ่งที่ปั้นไว้ต้มต่อไปจนสุก ยก
ลง ตักใส่ถ้วยรับประทานร้อนๆ หรือ
เย็นก็ได้

TARO BALLS IN COCONUT SYRUP

INGREDIENTS:

$\frac{1}{2}$ cup cooked, sieved taro root
1 cup rice flour
$\frac{1}{2}$ cup cornstarch
$1\frac{1}{2}$ cups water
2 cups sweet coconut milk
(see glossary)
2 tablespoons brown sugar
$\frac{1}{2}$ cup sugar
$\frac{1}{4}$ teaspoon salt
$\frac{1}{2}$ cup cornstarch
(for shaping balls)

METHOD:

Scrub, rinse and pare taro root.
Boil until tender, drain. Rub through
sieve or strainer into a mixing bowl.
Set aside.
In a saucepan dissolve rice flour
and cornstarch in $1\frac{1}{2}$ cups water.
Stir over low heat for 10 minutes
or until cooked. Remove to a flat
plate. Knead to a dough (moistening hands in cold water as necces-
sary.) Add the ground taro. Knead
again until well mixed. Form into
little balls about $\frac{1}{2}$ inch in diameter
(use cornstarch while shaping). In
another saucepan combine coconut
milk sugar, brown sugar, and salt.
Bring to the boiling point. Add the
prepared balls and continue boiling
for 10 — 15 minutes until they are
well cooked. Remove from heat.
Spoon into serving dish. Serve hot
or cold.

White Jelly with Fruit cocktail

This dessert is very popular in the summer. It is also interesting to note that one of the main ingredients is canned Fruit Cocktail. We only have canned fruit factory recently, therefore this dessert must have a lot of American influence, I suppose.

เต้าฮวยเย็น

ส่วน

วุ้นแท่ง	2 ออนซ์
	(วุ้นผง 1 ซอง)
นมข้นหวาน	½ ถ้วย
หัวน้ำมันอัลมอนด์	½ ช้อนชา
น้ำ	1 ถ้วย
ฟรุ๊ตสลัด	1 ถ้วย
น้ำแข็งทุบละเอียด	1 ถ้วย

วิธีทำ

แช่วุ้นในน้ำเย็นอย่างน้อย 10 นาที
ตั้งน้ำให้เดือด ใส่วุ้นคนเสมอจนวุ้น
ละลายดีแล้ว เติมนมข้นหวานคนจนเข้า
เนื้อกันดีใส่หัวน้ำหอมอัลมอนด์ เทใส่
พิมพ์ทิ้งไว้จนเย็นและแข็งดีแล้ว (ถ้า
จะให้เย็นเร็วใส่ช่องน้ำแข็ง) แกะออก
จากพิมพ์ใส่ชามแก้วใหญ่ ใส่น้ำเชื่อม
โรยหน้าด้วยฟรุ๊ตสลัดก่อนเสริฟ ใส่น้ำ
แข็งทุบไว้ตรงกลางหรือจะตักเสริฟเป็น
ถ้วยๆ ก็ได้

WHITE JELLY AND FRUIT COCKTAIL

INGREDIENTS:

1 package unsweetened
   gelatine   (1 tablespoon)
½ cup sweetened condensed
   milk
½ teaspoon almond extract
1 cup water
½ cup nam chuam syrup
                (see page 17)
1 cup fruit cocktail
1 cup cracked ice

METHOD:

Soak gelatine in ¼ cup cold water.
Combine with sweetened condensed
milk and water. Cook over low
heat until dissolved. Add almond
extract, stir well. Pour into wet, 1
quart mold or 6 individual cocktail
glasses. Chill until firm. Serve with
fruit cocktail and syrup topped
with cracked ice.

Fresh fruit in coconut syrup

This is another cool dessert for the summer. The coconut milk provides a tropical feel to the dish. Jasmine is very popular flower in Thailand. If you have been to Bangkok you would remember the jasmine leis which were everywhere, at the airport, the hotels, and the restaurants. I hope the smell of jasmine will remind you of Bangkok.

ผลไม้สดน้ำกะทิ

ส่วน

ฮันนี่ดิว(ใช้ช้อนตักเป็นลูกกลมๆ)	1 ถ้วย
แคนตาลูป (ตักเป็นลูกกลม)	1 ถ้วย
สับปะรด (ตักเป็นลูกกลมๆ)	½ ถ้วย
มะละกอ (ตักเป็นลูกกลมๆ)	½ ถ้วย
น้ำกะทิสด	1 ถ้วย
น้ำตาล	1 ปอนด์
น้ำ	2 ถ้วย
หัวน้ำหอมมะลิ	2-3 หยด
น้ำแข็งทุบละเอียด	2 ถ้วย

วิธีทำ

(น้ำเชื่อม)

ละลายน้ำตาลกับน้ำตั้งไฟหมั่นคนจนน้ำ
เชื่อมพอเริ่มเหนียวกรอง ทิ้งไว้จนเย็น
หยดด้วยหัวน้ำหอมดอกมะลิจัดผลไม้ใส่
ชามใหญ่ราดด้วยน้ำเชื่อม ราดด้วยน้ำ
กะทิสดโรยด้วยน้ำแข็ง หรือจะเสริฟที่
ละถ้วยก็ได้

FRESH FRUITS WITH COCONUT SYRUP

INGREDIENTS:

- 1 cup honeydew melon, scooped into balls
- 1 cup cantaloupe, scooped into balls
- ½ cup pineapple
- ½ cup papaya
- 1 cup coconut milk (see glossary)
- 1 pound sugar
- 2 cups water
- Few drops Jasmine extract (optional)
- 2 cups cracked ice

METHOD:

Scoop or dice your favorite fruit into small pieces. (Honey dew, cantaloupe, papaya, pineapple)

In a large pot dissolve sugar and water, boil for 15 minutes or until syrup is formed. if necessary, strain through cheesecloth. Cool (Drop in jasmine extract if you like the flavor of it. Stir well.)

Arrange the fruit in a serving bowl. Pour syrup over it. Top with coconut milk and cracked ice. (Or serve in small individual serving dishes.)

Orange in Syrup

There must be more than half a dozen different type of oranges (som) in Thailand. Tangerine is called green sweet som, parmelo is called Som-oh. Som klieng is juicy and sweet orange with green skin. Som jook is peeling orange, green skin with knob on top. Som chine is Chinese orange, like tangerine but with thicker and more brittle skin, easy to peel. As for Sunkist orange the Thai word is, of course, Som Sunkist. For this summer dessert you can use any kind of "Som" that is available to you.

ส้มลอยแก้ว

น้ำเชื่อม   2 ถ้วย

           (ดูวิธีทำหน้า 167)

ส้มซันคิส (แกะเป็นกลีบๆ) 10 ผล

น้ำแข็งทุบ   2 ถ้วย

กลีบกุหลาบ

วิธีทำ

แกะส้มออกเป็นกลีบใส่จานไว้ พอเสริฟ
ตักใส่ถ้วยราดด้วยน้ำเชื่อมโรยด้วยน้ำแข็ง

ORANGE IN SYRUP

INGREDIENTS:

     2 cups nam chuam syrup

                   (see page 17)

     3 cups orange sections, white
        membrane removed
        (10 oranges) and other fruits
        as desired.

     2 cups cracked ice
        some rose petals

METHOD:

Place the orange sections into
individual serving dishes. Pour
syrup over oranges.

Top with cracked ice and rosepetals.
Serve at once.

Mango and sticky rice

If you lived for over a year in Bangkok, or had you been lucky enough to arrive in Bangkok at the proper time of the year, you would have tasted the famous dish of mango and sticky rice. The special kind of mango that we have in Thailand cannot be found in the US, but the one we found in Hawaii is quite acceptable as a substitute, as you see in the illustration.

ข้าวเหนียวมะม่วง

ส่วน

ข้าวเหนียว	2	ถ้วย
หัวกะทิสด	1	ถ้วย
น้ำตาล	$\frac{1}{2}$	ถ้วย
เกลือ	1	ช้อนชา
มะม่วงสุก	5	ผล
หัวกะทิกวนไฟ	2	ช้อนโต๊ะ

วิธีทำ

ซาวข้าวเหนียวให้สะอาด เติมน้ำแช่ทิ้ง
ไว้ 5-8 ชั่วโมงเทข้าวเหนียวใส่ชามใหญ่
ใส่น้ำพอท่วม (น้ำท่วมข้าว $\frac{1}{2}$ นิ้ว) นึ่ง
ในรังถึงจนสุก (หรือจะใช้หุงในหม้อ
ข้าวไฟฟ้าก็ได้) เทลงในชามน้ำกะทิ
ผสมน้ำตาลเกลือกวนให้เข้ากัน บิดฝา
ไว้จนระอุดีเวลารับประทาน ปอกมะ
ม่วงจัดใส่จานไว้ข้างหนึ่ง ตักข้าวเหนียว
ไว้อีกข้างหนึ่ง ราดด้วยหัวกะทิที่กวนไฟ
เสริฟ

MANGO AND STICKY RICE

INGREDIENTS:
2 cups sticky rice (see glossary)
1 cup coconut milk
(see glossary)
$\frac{1}{2}$ cup sugar
1 teaspoon salt
5 medium yellow mangoes
2 tablespoons cooked coconut
milk

METHOD:
Cook 2 tablespoons coconut milk
over low heat. Set aside. Soak the
sticky rice in water for 5–8 hours.
Strain, and place the sticky rice in
top of a double boiler. Cover the
sticky rice with water (about $\frac{1}{2}$ inch
above rice). Cook for 25 minutes
or until done. In a mixing bowl
dissolve sugar and salt in coconut
milk, Add the cooked sticky rice
and stir until well mixed. Cover
and let stand for 15 minutes. Peel
the mangoes off the stone and slice.
Place on a serving plate. Spoon
the cooked sticky rice beside the
mango. Top with cooked coco
nut milk. Serve.

Golden silk threades

The following two sweets have been known in Thailand more than four hundred years. They were said to have come to Siam with the Portuguese traders (or was it the Dutch?). Whatever their origin, they have remained favorites of the Royal Court and the ordinary people alike all through the years. You may well find this to be your favorite also.

SWEET GOLDEN SILK THREADS

INGREDIENTS:

12 eggs (yolks only & 1 teaspoon thin white)
2 cups syrup (see page 17)
4–5 fine point paper cones

METHOD:

Separate eggs. Make sure to put egg white into one bowl and yolks into another. Put remaining egg white that you can scrape out with your finger from the shells, into a

ฝอยทอง

ส่วน

ไข่   12 ฟอง

น้ำเชื่อม (ดูหน้า 17)   2 ถ้วย

วิธีทำ

แยกไข่แดงและไข่ขาวไว้คนละทาง ใช้เฉพาะไข่แดงผสมไข่น้ำค้างสัก 1 ช้อนชา กรองด้วยผ้าขาวบาง

ตั้งน้ำเชื่อมบนไฟกลางๆ พอเดือด ใช้กรวยใบตองหรือ กระดาษเทียน (แบบทำหน้าขนมเค็ก) ตักไข่ใส่กรวยทีละน้อย โรยไข่ลงในน้ำเชื่อม วนมือ รอบๆหม้อ พอไข่หมดใช้ไม้แหลม หรือตะเกียบ ตักฝอยทองขึ้นพักไว้ในกระชอนให้น้ำเชื่อมไหลออกให้หมด โรยอีกจนหมดไข่ ต้องเติมน้ำร้อนทุกครั้งเพื่อมิให้น้ำตาลข้นเกินไป

หมายเหตุ ถ้าใช้กรวยกระดาษจะต้องเปลี่ยนกรวยทุกครั้ง

ทองหยิบ

ส่วน

เหมือนกับฝอยทองทุกอย่าง

วิธีทำ

ตั้งน้ำเชื่อมจนเดือด ยกออกจากเตา ตักไข่แดงทีละครึ่งช้อนโต๊ะ หยดลงในน้ำเชื่อมทีละ 5 หรือ 6 หยด ตั้งไฟอีก พอไข่สุกใช้ช้อนตักใส่จานแบน พออุ่นจีบเป็นจีบใส่ถ้วยตะไล หรือเปลือกไข่ ทำจนหมดไข่ ต้องเติมน้ำร้อนทุกครั้ง เพื่อมิให้น้ำเชื่อมข้นเกินไป

---

third bowl. Only 1 teaspoon of this thin egg white is needed. It is essential for the successful appearance of the "foi thong".

Strain the yolk and the thin egg white through a fine sieve. (The rest of the egg white can be used for another dish.)

In a saucepan heat the nam chuam syrup over mediun low heat. Pour about $\frac{1}{4}$ cup of the strained egg yolks into a fine point paper cone with your finger over the hole. Remove your finger. releasing the egg yolks in a regular stream into the boiling syrup, moving your hand very rapidly round and round the pan so that you get very fine but unbroken lines of the yellow. The egg strings cook very quickly so remove them almost at once with chopsticks or a slotted spoon. Add a little boiling water each time before repeating this process. (If the syrup is thick the Foi Thong will be crinkly).

GOLDEN EGG CAKE

INGREDIENTS:

The same as for "Foi Thong".

METHOD:

In a sauce pan heat syrup over medium heat. When syrup is boiling remove from heat. Spoon $\frac{1}{2}$ tablespoon egg yolk mixture and drop into the syrup, 5—6 drops at a time. Place the pan back on heat and cook until the yolk is done. Spoon onto a flat plate. Add a little hot water before repeating the drops. Shape the cooked yolk into a flower and place into a small cup or egg shell. Makes 25—30 flowers.

coconut pudding

You will have noticed by now that the coconut is used quite often as an important ingredient in Thai cooking. In Arizona, coconut milk can be ordered in a bottle with your **dairy** produce. I imagine it would be the same in other big cities. We use coconut milk here with the Thai style coconut pudding. If you do not have a banana leaf, any glass or ceramic cup will do.

ตะโก้

ส่วน

ตัว แห้วจีนปอกหั่นเป็นชิ้นเล็กๆ $\frac{1}{2}$ ถ้วย
(หรือเม็ดบัวต้ม $\frac{1}{2}$ ถ้วย)

แป้งข้าวเจ้า	$\frac{1}{2}$	ถ้วย
แป้งข้าวโพด	$\frac{1}{4}$	ถ้วย
น้ำ	1	ถ้วย
น้ำตาลสีรำ	1	ช้อนโต๊ะ
น้ำตาลทราย	1	ถ้วย
สีแดง	2-3	หยด
หน้า น้ำกะทิหวาน	1 $\frac{1}{2}$	ถ้วย
แป้งข้าวเจ้า	1	ช้อนโต๊ะ
แป้งข้าวโพด	1 $\frac{1}{2}$	ช้อนโต๊ะ
เกลือ	1	ช้อนชา
กลีบกุหลาบ		

วิธีทำ

ตัว ใช้ชามก้นลึก ละลายแป้งข้าวเจ้า, แป้งข้าวโพด, น้ำ, สีแดง และน้ำตาลสีรำกับน้ำตาลทราย กรองด้วยกระชอนเทลงในหม้อ ตั้งไฟกลางๆ กวนจนแป้งสุก ลดไฟกวนต่อไปอีก 5 นาที ใส่แห้วหรือเม็ดบัวต้ม กวนจนเข้าเนื้อดี ตักใส่ถ้วยเล็กๆหรือกระทง, หรือถ้วยกระดาษ(ถ้าใส่ถ้วยกระดาษต้องรองในถาดสำหรับอบคัพเค็ก) พักไว้

หน้า ละลายน้ำกะทิหวาน กับแป้งข้าวเจ้า, แป้งข้าวโพดและเกลือ กรอง, ตั้งไฟอ่อนๆกวนจนสุก หมั่นคนอย่าให้เป็นลูก ยกลง ตักหยอดลงบนตัวขนมทุกถ้วย พักไว้พอเย็นโรยด้วยกลีบกุหลาบ

COCONUT PUDDING

INGREDIENTS:

BOTTOM LAYER

$\frac{1}{2}$ cup water chestnuts chopped
fine or

$\frac{1}{4}$ cup cooked dried lotus seeds

$\frac{1}{2}$ cup rice flour

$\frac{1}{4}$ cup cornstarch

1 cup water

1 tablespoon light brown sugar

1 cup sugar

2-3 drops red food coloring
(optional)

TOP LAYER 1$\frac{1}{2}$ cups sweet coconut
milk (see glossary)

1 tablespoon rice flour

1$\frac{1}{2}$ tablespoons cornstarch

1 teaspoon salt
rose petals

METHOD:

BOTTOM LAYER; Mix together: rice flour, cornstarch, light brown sugar, 2-3 drops red food coloring and water; strain through strainer into a saucepan. Stir over medium low heat until well cooked. Lower the heat and continue stirring, and cook for 5 minutes more. Remove from heat. Spoon into small cups or banana leaf cups. Set aside.

TOP LAYER: Blend rice flour and cornstarch with sweet coconut milk. Add salt and stir over medium low heat until thickened. Spoon the white mixture over the pink mixture. Cool. Garnish with rose petals.

Kanom Tom Kanom Niew

See Indonesian
pp 286 for dough

ขนมต้ม ขนมเหนียว

ส่วน

มะพร้าวใช้ฝาเบียร์ขูดเป็น
เส้น ๆ   1/2 ถ้วย
น้ำตาลสีรำ   2 ช้อนโต๊ะ
เกลือ   1/2 ช้อนชา
มะพร้าวขูดละเอียด (ใช้ที่ขูด
ผิวมะนาวขูด)   1 ½ ถ้วย
แป้งข้าวเหนียว   2 ถ้วย
น้ำ   1 ถ้วย
สีเขียว 2 หยด สีเหลือง 1 หยด
หรือน้ำใบเตย

**KANOM TOM KANOM NIEW
(GLUTINOUS RICE FLOUR BALLS
WITH COCONUT FILLING)**

INGREDIENTS :

1/2 cup flaked coconut (use bottle cap to grate)

2 tablespoos brown sugar

1 teaspoon salt

1-1/2 cup grated coconut

2 cups glutinous rice flour

1 cup water

2 drops green, one drop yellow food coloring

2 tablespoons rice crispy

1/4 cup maple honey syrup

ข้าวคั่ว   2 ช้อนโต๊ะ

น้ำผึ้ง เมเปิลไซรับ 1/2 ถ้วย

วิธีทำ ผสมมะพร้าวขูดเส้น ๆ น้ำตาล
สีรำ เกลือ ลงในกะทะตั้งไฟกวนพอ
แห้ง เป็นหน้ากะฉีก พักไว้ พอเย็น
ปั้นเป็นก้อนกลม ๆ เส้นผ่าศูนย์กลาง
1/2 นิ้ว พักไว้

        ผสมมะพร้าวขูดละเอียด ผสม
เกลือนิดหน่อย นึ่ง พักไว้

        ผสมแป้งข้าวเหนียว   กับน้ำ
และสีทั้งสองสี   นวดให้เข้ากันดีแล้ว
แบ่งแป้งเป็นก้อนกลม ๆ เส้นผ่าศูนย์
กลาง 1 นิ้ว แผ่ให้แบน ใส่ไส้กะฉีก
หุ้มให้มิดไส้   ทำจนหมดไส้จะได้ขนม
ต้มประมาณ 30 ลูก ตั้งน้ำพอเดือด
ใส่ขนมต้มลงไป   พอขนมสุกจะลอย
ขึ้นมา   ตักขึ้นเคล้ากับมะพร้าวขูดให้
ทั่ว จัดใส่จาน

        ส่วนแป้งที่เหลือ แผ่เป็นแท่ง
ยาว ๆ บนกระดาษเทียน   ตัดเป็นชิ้น ๆ
เท่านิ้วก้อย   แล้วต้มพอแป้งสุก ลอย
ขึ้นมาตักเคล้ากับมะพร้าวขูด   จัดใส่จาน
โรยด้วยข้าวคั่ว   เสริฟกับน้ำตาลไหม้
น้ำผึ้ง-เมเปิลไซรับ

หมายเหตุ น้ำตาลไหม้ ใช้น้ำตาลสีรำ
1/4 ถ้วย เทลงในกะทะตั้งไฟพอเป็น
ฟอง เติมน้ำสุก 1/4 ถ้วย คนพอละ
ลาย เทใส่ถ้วย

METHOD :

        In a pan mix together coconut flakes
and brown sugar, cook over low heat.
Stir constantly until almost dry. Cool,
shape into small balls of 1/2" diameter.
Make 30 balls.

        Steam grated coconut, mix with
a little salt to prevent the coconut from
going sour. Set aside.

        Put glutinous rice flour in a bowl.
Add water, 2 colors food coloring and
mix well. Take a small lump of dough,
about one inch diameter, flatten it, put
a coconut ball in the middle and roll
into a ball. Repeat until all coconut balls
are used up. Boil a pot of water. Drop
glutionous rice balls into boiling water.
Remove when they rise to the surface.
Drain and roll in steamed grated coconut.
Cut the leftover dough into small strips,
then drop into boiling water. Remove
when they rise to the surface. Drain
and roll in the steamed grated coconut.
Arrange onto serving plate, top with
rice cripsy and maple honey syrup.

NOTE :   To make rice cripsy, clean the
rice and brown in the frying pan without
oil until light brown.

Seaweed Jelly

Jellies are quite popular as Thai desserts. There are many ways to prepare them. I have two suggestions which give you quite different results. For Easter, my suggestion for using egg shells as a mold should prove popular with the children.

วุ้น

ส่วน วุ้นสาหร่าย แช่น้ำ 1-2 ชั่วโมง

2 ถ้วย

น้ำ   4 ถ้วย

น้ำตาล   2 ถ้วย

SEAWEED JELLY

INGREDIENTS :

2 cups seaweed jelly

4 cups water

2 cups sugar

3/4 cup golden silk threads

(see page 172)

ฝอยทอง (ดูหน้า 173)   2 แพ

น้ำกะทิ   2 ถ้วย

น้ำตาล   1/2 ถ้วย

เกลือ   1 ช้อนชา

แป้งมัน   1 ช้อนชา

สือาหาร แห้วจีนหรือมันแกว หรือลูก
แพดิบ เปลือกไข่ กลีบกุหลาบ ใบเตย

วิธีทำ เคี่ยววุ้น กับน้ำ จนละลาย, ใส่
น้ำตาล หรี่ไฟ เคี่ยวต่อไปอีก 10-15
นาที กรองด้วยกระชอน แบ่งเป็น 2
ส่วน ตั้งไฟอ่อน ๆ

ส่วนที่หนึ่ง วุ้นกะทิ ผสมกะทิ
น้ำตาล เกลือ แป้งมัน ใบเตยตั้งไฟ
คนพอสุก ตักใบเตยออก ผสมเข้าด้วย
กันกับวุ้นส่วนที่ 1 แล้วเทใส่ถาด ทิ้ง
ไว้ พอเย็นตัดด้วยพิมพ์คุ้กกี้ ประดับ
ด้วยกลีบกุหลาบ

ส่วนที่สอง วุ้นสายทอง หยด
สีเหลืองลง 1 หยด คนพอละลาย เท
ใส่ถาดขนาด 6 ½ X 10” ใส่ฝอย
ทองแล้วเขี่ยให้ทั่วทิ้งไว้จนเย็น   ตัด
เป็นรูป 4 เหลี่ยมขนมเปียกปูนหรือ
ใช้พิมพ์คุ้กกี้ตัดก็ได้ ตบแต่งด้วยฝอย
ทอง

หรือ ส่วนหนึ่งจะผสมสี แดง
หรือ เขียว เทใส่พิมพ์ หรือเปลือกไข่
แล้วสลักมันแกว แห้วจีน หรือ ลูกแพ
เป็นดอกไม้ ตบแต่งก็ได้

2 cups coconut milk

1/2 cup sugar

1 teaspoon salt

1 teaspoon cornstarch

food coloring

green pear, water chestnuts or yam

egg shells, rose petals

METHOD

Soak seaweed jelly in water for one
hour. Drain and measure. Boil 4 cups
water in a sauce pan. Dissolve the seaweed jelly in it. Add sugar and boil for
15 minutes. Pour one half into one pan
and return to low heat. Pour the remaining half into a 6-1/2 ''x 10'' plate;
add 1 drop of yellow food coloring;
top with golden silk threads; allow to
sit. Cut into squares. Garnish with the
remaining golden silk threads.

Blend constarch, sugar, salt with
coconut milk. Stir over medium low heat
until it comes to a boil. Add the cooked
seaweed jelly. Keep stirring and simmer
for 2-3 minutes. Pour into 7-1/2'' X 12''
plate. Cool. Cut with cookie cutters.
Garnish with rose petals.

NOTE :

Another method : Add a drop of red
or green food coloring to cooked seaweed jelly. Stir and pour into small
jelly molds or clean egg shells. Garnish
with small pieces of water chestnuts,
yam or green pear. If you use egg shells
as molds, before breaking the shell for
serving, dip it in warm water for a few
minutes. This will help to peel the shell
more easily.

Blue Sapphire

A few years ago when my husband worked with an airline, he was made acting manager of a travel company called Blue Sapphire. Though the airline and the travel company are now only a memory, I like the name of Blue Sapphire enough to use it here.

We use blue coloring here to match the name. You may use red coloring and call your creation Red Ruby. There is almost no limit to the variations, only do not forget to mention that you get the idea from this book.

ไพลินกรอบ

ส่วน

ลูกแพดิบ หั่นเป็นลูกเต๋าเล็ก ๆ
                                      1 ถ้วย

สีอาหาร สีฟ้า   3-5 หยด

แป้งมัน   1 ถ้วย

หัวกะทิ   1 ถ้วย

น้ำเชื่อม (ดูหน้า 17)   1 ถ้วย

ขนุนสด   หรือกระป๋องหั่น

สี่ เหลี่ยม   1/2 ถ้วย

น้ำแข็งทุบหรือน้ำแข็งใส

วิธีทำ

เคล้าสีฟ้ากับลูกแพหั่นให้เข้า
กันดีจนสีเสมอกัน ใส่แป้งมันลงใน
ถุงปลาสติก ใส่ลูกแพหั่นลงไป รัด
ปากถุงให้แน่น เขย่าจนแป้งติดชิ้นของ
ลูกแพ เทลงใส่จาน แยกเม็ดที่ติด
ออกจากกัน ต้มน้ำพอเดือด ใส่เมล็ด
แป้งลงไป   พอสุกเม็ดจะลอยขึ้นมา
เทใส่กระชอนพอสะเด็ดน้ำ ใส่น้ำ
แข็งใช้มือแยกเมล็ดไพลินกรอบออก
จากกัน เทใส่ในน้ำกะทิสด แช่ไว้ใน
ตู้เย็น เสริฟในชามแก้วใส ใส่น้ำเชื่อม
และขนุน ใส่น้ำแข็งใส หรือใส่น้ำแข็ง
ทุบก็ได้

BLUE SAPPHIRE

INGREDIENTS :

    1 cup green pear cut into small dice

    3-5 drops blue food coloring

    1 cup cornstarch

    1 cup coconut milk

    1 cup syrup (see page 17)

    1/2 cup diced jack fruit, fresh or
canned (optional)

    1 cup crushed ice.

METHOD :

    In a bowl mix diced pear and blue
coloring until color is even. Put the
cornstarch in large plastic bag. Add
blue diced pear. Shake well. Pour back
into the bowl. Use your fingers to separate them. Then pour into boiling water.
When they rise to the surface, put into
strainer. Add ice to make it set. Drain
and place in bowl. Pour the coconut
milk over. Refrigerate until ready to serve.
Spoon the blue sapphire into individual
serving dishes. Pour syrup over. Garnish
with diced jack fruit. Top with crushed
ice. Serve at once.

Orange and Grapefruit Skin Preserve

The hardest part of this recipe is to prepare the skin properly. You should grate off the outer cover of the skin using cheese grater or small carving knife.

For variations, the preserve may be chopped up to mix with fruit cake, upside down cake, or apple pie fillings. The skin is used as a by-product, it does not cost anything after you consume the fruit. Of course I am not counting the sugar and the manpower or woman power to make this preserve, you do this in your spare time anyway, right?

เปลือกส้มแช่อิ่ม

ส่วน เปลือกส้มโอหรือเปลือกเกรฟ
พรุ้ทสีชมพู 1 ลูก
เปลือกส้ม Sunkist 2 ลูก
เปลือกมะนาว 1 ลูก
น้ำ-ตาล 3 ถ้วย
น้ำ 1 ถ้วย
น้ำปูนใส

วิธีทำ ปอกเปลือกส้มโอ หรือ เกรฟ
พรุ้ท แล้วหั่นเป็นชิ้นสี่เหลี่ยม ฝนผิว
ส้มเอาผิวออกบ้างเล็กน้อย (ใช้ที่ฝน
เนยแข็ง อันถี่ที่สุด) แล้วผ่าเป็นหก
ปอกใช้แต่เปลือก ฝนผิวมะนาวเช่น
เดียวกับผิวส้ม แบ่ง-4 แล้วลอกใช้แต่
เปลือก แช่ผิวส้มทั้งหมดในน้ำปูนใส
1 ชั่วโมง แล้วต้มในน้ำเดือด ประ-
มาณ 10 นาที หรือพอสุกตักผิวส้ม
ใส่น้ำเย็นบีบให้แห้ง เติมน้ำ แล้วบีบ
อีก 2 ครั้ง จนหมดความขม ผึ่งไว้ให้
แห้ง ผสมน้ำ 1 ถ้วย กับน้ำตาล 2 ½
ถ้วย ตั้งไฟเคี่ยวจะน้ำตาลขันใส่ผิว
ส้ม Sunkist และผิวมะนาวก่อนเชื่อม
ประมาณ 5 นาที ไฟอ่อน ๆ ตักขึ้นใส่
จาน ใส่ผิวส้มโอลงไป น้ำจะแห้ง ใช้
ช้อนใหญ่ หรือพายกวนต่อไปอีกประ-
มาณ 5 นาที โรยน้ำตาลที่เหลือลงไป
ให้ทั่วคนจนน้ำตาลละลาย ตักใส่จาน
พักไว้พอเย็นเก็บใส่ขวดโหล ใช้หั่น
เป็นชิ้นเล็กโรยบนไอสกรีมก็ได้ หรือ
รับประทานกับน้ำชาจีนก็ดี เก็บไว้ได้
นาน

ORANGE AND GRAPEFRUIT SKIN PRESERVE

INGREDIENTS :

2 oranges (sunkist)
1 grapefruit (pink)
1 lemon
Cold water
2 1/2 cups sugar
1/2 cup sugar for sprinkle

METHOD :

Rub off the orange peel lightly.
Then cut an orange into sixths, using
only the skin; makes 12 pieces. Do the
same with lemon but cut into fourths.
Peel the grapefruit peel off, cut the
skin into small squares. Cook all skins
in boiling water for 10-15 minutes or
until done. Drain and place in cold water.
Remove and squeeze till dry, place in
a bowl with new water. Repeat squeezing
three times until bitter tastle is gone
from the skins. In a sauce pan boil the
sugar and water until it thickens. Add
orange grapefruit and lemon skins.
Cook for 5 minutes more. Stir constantly
for 5 minutes; sprinkle top with sugar.
Stir until sugar is dissolved. Spoon into
a plate. Cool for 1 hour. Keep in a tightly
closed jar. Serve as topping for ice cream.
It is also good with hot tea.

American Fruit Tray

When we moved to Jakarta in 1977, our family enjoyed the greenest capital we have ever seen. Anywhere you look, there are trees. It reminded us of our great King Chulalongkorn who once said that in Java, if you put your walking stick into the ground, it will grow up to be a tree. We found Jack Fruit, banana and Salak to be very good but alas, the other fruits are not comparable to those in Thailand or America. By the time you read this we should have been back in Bangkok, since January 1980, and able to enjoy our best fruit, the durian.

ถาดผลไม้อเมริกัน

ผลไม้ที่หาง่ายทุกฤดูในอเมริกา ก็คือ ส้ม ลูกแพ และแอปเปิ้ล ลองปอกและสลักแบบง่าย เสริฟเป็นของหวานได้ วิธีทำง่าย ๆ ดังนี้

รูปที่ 1 ส้ม ผ่าออกเป็นแปด ค่อย ๆ ปอกเปลือกออกมาแล้วใช้กรรไกรขลิบดังรูปภาพ

รูปที่ 2 แอ็ปเปิลและลูกแพ ใช้มีดทองหั่นเป็นหกหรือแปดชิ้น แล้วปอกเปลือกอีกที ข้อสำคัญคือต้องใช้มะนาวทาที่ผิว แอ็ปเปิลหรือลูกแพทันที มิฉะนั้นจะดำ แล้วใช้กรรไกรขลิบแบบเดิม แช่น้ำผสมมะนาวเล็กน้อย ประมาณ 5 นาที หยิบขึ้นใส่จานแช่ตู้เย็นไว้จนกว่าจะเสริฟ

AMERICAN FRUIT TRAY

We choose here some fruits most popular in America. We can do some simple carving on Pear, Apple, Tangerine and Orange.

In figure 1, gently cut the skin of tangerine or orange into eight sectors. Peel down the skin equally. Trim with scissor into leaf form as shown in the drawing.

Figure 2 for Pear and Apple. Cut into six or eight portions. Peal the skin with carving knife to make a leaf form as above. Use scissor to trim into final shape.

Important : You must use lime or lemon to rub the exposed fruit portions immediately after cutting to prevent the fruit from turning black. After trimming of leaf, dip the fruit portions into water-lemon solution for five minutes. Take out of the water and arrange on serving tray. Keep in the refrigerator until ready to serve.

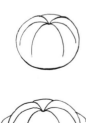

Mock Jack Fruit Seeds

The real seed of the Jack fruit is normally more than three fourths of an inch long. The seeds are very delicious when boiled in plain water. A little salt should be added to sharpen the taste. It is very difficult sometimes to decide which is better, the real Jack Fruit Seeds or the Mock seeds that we have here. Fortunately, we can enjoy both of them since the Mock Jack Fruit Seeds do not require any part of the real seed to make.

เม็ดขนุน

ส่วน

ถั่วเขียว หรือ ถั่วทอง	1 ถ้วย
มะพร้าวขูด	1 ถ้วย
น้ำตาลทราย	3/4 ถ้วย
เกลือ	1 ช้อนชา

ไข่แดง 5 ฟอง และไข่น้ำค้าง
1 ช้อนชา
น้ำเชื่อม (ดูหน้า 17) 2 ถ้วย

วิธีทำ

แช่ถั่วเขียวไว้หนึ่งคืน ลอก
เปลือกออก แล้วต้มจนเปื่อย เซ็ดน้ำ
แล้วบด (ใช้ที่ Mash patato) พอละเอียด
ผสมเข้าด้วยกันกับมะพร้าวขูด น้ำตาล
และเกลือ เคล้าจนเข้ากันดี ใส่กะทะ
กวนจนแห้ง พอเย็น ปั้นเป็นก้อนกลม
รี คล้ายเม็ดขนุน จะได้ประมาณ 30-
40 เม็ด

แยกไข่แดงและไข่ขาว ไว้คน
ละทาง ผสมไข่น้ำค้าง ใช้ซ่อมตีเบา ๆ
จนเข้ากันดี แล้วใส่เม็ดขนุนลงไป ครั้ง
10 เม็ด ตั้งน้ำเชื่อม พอเดือดยกลง
ใช้ช้อนตักเม็ดขนุนชุบไข่ลงในน้ำเชื่อม
ทีละเม็ดจนหมด ตั้งไฟอีก พอสุกตัก
เรียงใส่จาน ทำเช่นนี้จนหมด

MOCK JACK FRUIT SEEDS

INGREDIENTS :

1 cup skinned green bean; washed,
soaked overnight and drained

1 cup grafed coconut

3/4 cup sugar

1 teaspoon salt

5 eggs (yolks only, one tablespoon
thin clear white)

2 cups syrup (see page 17)

METHOD :

Cook the green beans with a little water until soft. Mash. Add grated
coconut, sugar and salt. Mix well, place
into a pan and cook over low heat until
almost dry. Cool and shape into small
ovals. It will make about 30-40 seeds.

Into the sauce pan heat the syrup
over medium heat. When syrup is boiling
remove from heat. Dip the seeds in the
yolks and drop in hot syrup one by one,
ten at a time. Place the pan back on
heat and cook until the yolk is done.
Spoon on to a plate.

Repeat until all the seeds are finished.

Simple Fruit Carving

We have in Thailand probably the largest number of fruits that are available all year round. The Thais like fruits and they find many ways to preserve and to cook them for desserts. For fresh consumption they carve the fruit before serving. There are many good books written on fruit and vegetable carving. I show here only the most simple method that can be applied to fruits readily found in American supermarkets.

สลัก ผลไม้สดในอเมริกา

ผลไม้เป็นของหวานของคน
ไทยมาตลอดเวลา เวลาเสริฟผลไม้
เรามักจะปอก จัด สลักเสลา ให้น่า
รับประทาน ขอเสนอวิธีสลักผลไม้
ง่าย ๆ ดังนี้
รูปที่ 1 กระเช้าแตงโม หรือ อาจจะ
       เป็น แคนตารูฟ ฮันนี่ดิว หรือ
       เกรฟพรุ้ทลูกใหญ่ก็ได้
รูปที่ 2 ใบไม้ทำด้วย มะละกอ แคน-
       ตารูฟ หรือ แตงโม

SIMPLE FRUIT CARVING

Some fruit can be carved and served without much labour. Two ways of preparation are shown here.

In figure 1 :

Watermelon, Cantaloupe or Honeydew Melon Basket

Step 1 : Keep the stemside up. Mark the handle with point of knife.

Step 2 : Cut across the sides of the melon first and then cut from the top down. Remove the cut portion carefully.

Step 3 : Carve the design of your choice on the skin and handle. The pulp can be removed from the basket by using scooping spoon. When you finish re-fill it with balls of the melon or other fruits.

In figure 2 : Papaya or Cantaloupe Leaves

Step 1 : Peel and cut into heart shape.

Step 2 : Outline the middle vein and carve a zig-zag around the leaf.

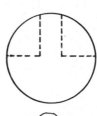

189

Sticky Rice Ball

Glutinous rice is prepared in many different ways. We have seen it made with chicken and we have seen it served with mango. It can be prepared on its own to taste quite delicious in the following recipe. The Thai name for this sweet rice is called "Sticky Crystal Rice".

ข้าวเหนียวแก้ว

ส่วน

ข้าวเหนียว	
หัวกะทิ	1 ถ้วย
น้ำตาลทราย	1 ถ้วย
เกลือ	1 ช้อนชา
สีขนม	

วิธีทำ

ซาวข้าวเหนียวให้สะอาด เท
น้ำร้อนใส่พอท่วม คนให้เข้ากันแช่ทิ้ง
ไว้ 10 นาที แล้วนึ่งในรังถึงที่ปูด้วย
ผ้าขาวบาง ประมาณ 25-30 นาที พอ
สุกผึ่งให้เย็น

กวนกะทิ น้ำตาล เกลือ บน
ไฟอ่อน ๆ พอน้ำตาลละลาย ใส่ข้าว
เหนียวลงไปแล้วกวนจนแห้ง แบ่งใส่
ชามเท่า ๆ กัน 3 ชาม ชามที่ 1 ใส่
แดง 3 หยด ชามที่ 2 ใส่สีเขียว 2 หยด
สีเหลือง 1 หยด ชามที่สามไม่ใส่สี
พอเย็นปั้นเป็นก้อนกลม ๆ เรียงใส่
ชาม สลับสีให้สวยงาม

หมายเหตุ สีน้ำตาล ใช้น้ำตาลสีรำ
แทนน้ำตาลทราย

STICKY RICE BALLS

INGREDIENTS :

    2 cups sticky rice (see glossary)
    1 cup coconut milk (see glossary)
    1 cup sugar
    1 teaspoon salt
    food coloring

METHOD :

Soak the sticky rice in hot water
for 10 minutes and steam for 25 minutes
or until done. Cool.

Into a deep pan put coconut milk,
sugar and salt; cook over low heat until sugar is dissolved. Add sticky rice,
stir constantly and cook until almost
dry. Separate into 3 equal portions. Add
to each portion a different food coloring
and stir until the color is even. Shape
into small balls. Arrange on a serving
plate.

NOTE :

For brown Sticky Rice Balls, you
may use brown sugar instead of regular
white sugar to get the desired color.

40 YEARS OF MASTER BREWING

SINGHA BEER